"This is a remarkable and timely book: ~~thoughtful, funny, and elegant.~~

  – **Michael Coren**, author, broadcaster, and journalist

"Andy Bannister's book is a breath, a gust, a positive whoosh of fresh air. Made me laugh, made me think, made me cry. The words bounce across the page. A sane Christian! Whatever next?"

  – **Adrian Plass**, author and speaker

"Every atheist vs believer debate I've been to has made me want to gouge out my eyes with a spoon. Bannister's book, however, is exactly what this sceptical believer needed."

  – **Drew Marshall**, radio host

"In a brilliant work that is as humorous as it is damaging to atheist arguments, Bannister demonstrates the consequences of implementing New Atheist arguments in real life (that is, out of the realm of stuffy office speculations). His work is a wild ride that takes the reader from stories to theory to end game. Writing with eloquence and imagination, he illustrates the supposed 'safe ground' of New Atheist thought as truly no ground at all."

  – **Professor Mary Jo Sharp**, Houston Baptist University

"Andy Bannister provides a set of powerful and accessible arguments that can be used by ordinary people in responding to the tsunami of atheist sound bites flooding public discourse in the West. His tongue-in-cheek humour gives a certain lightness which does not in any way undermine the rigour and force of the book's arguments. This is not a negative study – though atheism is certainly taken to the cleaners – and it is also profoundly positive in presenting compelling arguments for the central claims of Christianity."

  – **Dr Peter Riddell**, Professorial Research Associate, History, SOAS, University of London

"A book that tackles heady things with humour and grace and in a way that ordinary people like myself can actually understand. Highly recommended; I read it twice!"

– Jeff Allen, comedian

"This lively, witty, and engaging book provides a powerful and thoughtful critique of the New Atheism associated with Richard Dawkins and others. This is a lovely book, which draws deeply on high-quality philosophical, historical, and scientific thinking. A readable, thoughtful, and humorous challenge to those who hold New Atheist beliefs. Highly recommended!"

– Professor Steve Walton, St Mary's University, London

"This book is for you, whether you're an atheist, a doubter, or a believer. In an age of overdone rhetoric that lacks substance, Andy Bannister has done what few writers on the topic of God have done: made it fun and fast-paced, yet fair and sincere. Andy has the rare ability to use humour to expose the faulty logic of bad arguments while at the same time being respectful to the people who might use those same arguments. You'll laugh in these pages even as your intellect is stimulated and your thinking is challenged. The Atheist Who Didn't Exist is a thoughtful book that will stimulate the humour and intelligence of the atheists who do exist. I wholeheartedly recommend it!"

– Abdu Murray, speaker and author of Grand Central Question: Answering the Critical Concerns of the Major Worldviews

"It's the 'God Debate', but not as you know it. In this conversational, well-researched and accessible volume, Andy Bannister offers an intelligent, provocative, and humorous engagement with the New Atheism. Andy asks big questions and challenges some dominant assumptions. Share and enjoy."

– Paul Woolley, Deputy Chief Executive, Bible Society

"I would especially highlight this book's accessibility. Although it is well endowed with references, its populist, racy style may well appeal to readers who would be unlikely to engage with yet another 'academic' treatise on faith and secularism. On these grounds, I recommend it as an important addition to the debate on the most fundamental issue confronting any person, anywhere, at any time: are there good grounds for believing in a God or are believers such as Christians suffering delusional irrationality? This book may help each reader to come to a conclusion based on argumentation and evidence presented with satirical humour: a very valuable addition to the library!"

– Baroness Caroline Cox, founder of Humanitarian Aid Relief Trust

"This is the most enjoyable critique of popular atheism I have read. It is serious fun, by which I mean it somehow offers deeply thoughtful responses to modern scepticism while regularly making you laugh – often laughing at Andy's true wit, sometimes at that 'British drollery'! Oddly, for such an entertaining riposte to fashionable atheist arguments, the book is remarkably free of smugness and self-congratulation. I could – and will – give this book to my sceptical friends."

– Dr John Dickson, Founding Director of the Centre for Public Christianity, and Honorary Fellow of the Department of Ancient History, Macquarie University

About the Author

Dr Andy Bannister is the Director of RZIM Canada. He speaks and teaches regularly throughout Canada, the USA, Europe, and the wider world. From universities to churches, business forums to TV and radio, Andy regularly addresses audiences of all faiths and none on issues relating to faith, culture, politics, and society.

Andy holds a PhD in Islamic Studies, a topic on which he has taught extensively, especially since 9/11 and the huge interest that was sparked in the subject by the events of that day. He has spoken and taught at universities across Canada, the USA, the UK, and further afield on both Islam and philosophy, and is an Adjunct Research Fellow at the Centre for the Study of Islam and Other Faiths at Melbourne School of Theology. He is also author of *An Oral-Formulaic Study of the Qur'an*. He has a substantial following on Twitter: @andygbannister

When not travelling, speaking, or writing, Andy is a keen hiker, mountain climber, and photographer. He lives in Toronto with his family.

The Atheist Who Didn't Exist

Or: The Dreadful Consequences of Bad Arguments

ANDY BANNISTER

MONARCH
BOOKS

Oxford, UK, and Grand Rapids, Michigan, USA

Published by Monarch Books
an imprint of
Lion Hudson plc
Wilkinson House, Jordan Hill Road,
Oxford OX2 8DR, England
Email: monarch@lionhudson.com
www.lionhudson.com/monarch

ISBN 978 0 85721 610 6
e-ISBN 978 0 85721 611 3

First edition 2015

Acknowledgments
Unless otherwise indicated, Scripture quotations are taken from The Holy
Bible, New International Version Anglicised. Copyright © 1979, 1984, 2011
Biblica, formerly International Bible Society. All rights reserved. Anglicised
edition first published in Great Britain 1979 by Hodder & Stoughton, a
Hachette UK company. This revised and updated edition published 2011.

Scripture quotation marked KJV is taken from The Authorized (King
James) Version: rights in the Authorized Version in the United Kingdom are
vested in the Crown. Reproduced by permission of the Crown's patentee,
Cambridge University Press.

Further acknowledgments on page 237–38.

A catalogue record for this book is available from the British Library

Printed and bound in the UK, January 2016, LH26

In Memoriam
Peter Hicks (1940–2013)

"Who holds that if way to the Better there be, it exacts a full look at the Worst."

Thomas Hardy, *In Tenebris II*

Contents

Foreword

Two Australian sailors staggered out of a London pub into a dense fog and looked around for help. As they steadied themselves they saw a man walking into the pub, but evidently missed the military medals flashing on his uniform. One sailor blurted out: "Hey, mate, do you know where we are?"

The officer, thoroughly offended, snarled back: "Do you men know who I am?"

The sailors looked at each other, and one said to the other: "We're really in a mess now. We don't know where we are, and he doesn't know who he is."

Humorous as this scene may be, I would suggest that, without God as our ultimate frame of reference, we don't know who we are in essence or where we are in the grand scheme of life. As an atheist, you may counter that you don't need God and that belief in God is illogical. In fact, I have spoken at hundreds of university open forums for over forty years – and in nearly every setting I have encountered an atheist who charges Christianity with being irrational or, worse, poisonous to society. And yet, as we talk, time and again the atheist is unable to answer the fundamental questions of life, such as, "Is there a moral framework to life?" To be sure, they keep trying, but there is a difference between offering a pragmatic explanation and all the while being unable to anchor it in logical inescapabilty.

There are serious questions of life that have to be faced by every world view, and each of us must think through our arguments carefully rather than resort to clever sound bites or shouting. My colleague Andy Bannister offers us an invitation to do just this, wisely showing, for example, that we learn to tell a bad argument from a good one when we test the argument in a different setting. Andy is a brilliant and winsome communicator who relishes a good conversation – but, more importantly, loves the person he is engaging with. It is an honour for me to work with him as a teammate.

This is a very witty but altogether serious book that shouldn't be taken lightly lest we miss the ultimate questions at stake. I know you will enjoy reading it, and I heartily recommend it.

Ravi Zacharias, author and speaker

The Loch Ness Monster's Moustache

(or: The Terrible Consequences of Bad Arguments)

I remember the first time that I saw *the* bus. An old friend of mine had telephoned me out of the blue a few days before, and in a conspiratorial whisper had hissed: "You need to get down to London. There are *atheist* buses here."

"Atheist buses?" I replied, bleary-eyed. It was long past midnight. "How much have you drunk, Tom?"

"Only four pints," Tom replied indignantly.

"Well, I've always personally thought that the slightly devil-may-care attitude of many London bus drivers to road safety tends to bring people *closer* to God, rather than drive them away."

"This bus didn't try to drive me away; it tried to drive *over* me. Admittedly, I was lying semi-comatose in the road at the time – "

"I *knew* it!"

" – at Hammersmith, and the atheist bus almost ran me over."

"You do realize", I explained, in the patient tone I reserve for small children and airline check-in agents, "that just because a London bus almost flattens a liberal Anglican lying on a zebra crossing, it doesn't necessarily mean that Richard Dawkins is resorting to hit-and-run attempts to keep the religious affiliation statistics favourable."

"I'm used to being nearly run over, I've holidayed in France many times,"[1] snapped Tom. "But this was an *atheist* bus, I tell you."

"You're sure about this?"

"Yes! Now come down to London and see. Besides, you owe me a beer from that time when you lost the bet about the Archbishop's beard."[2]

And so it was that I found myself, on a rainy July afternoon a few weeks later, standing among a crowd of damp tourists outside Oxford Circus tube station. We watched the traffic as cars, taxis, lorries, and the occasional sodden cyclist trundled past. And then, at last, a bus rounded the corner. A big, red London bus sporting a huge advertisement on the side, which announced in large friendly letters: "There's Probably No God. Now Stop Worrying and Enjoy Your Life."

Later, back in the comfort of a nearby pub, I did a little research.[3] It turned out that the bus advertisements had been sponsored by The British Humanist Association along with a group of secular celebrities, including the well-known Oxford

---

1   It has been remarked that you can tell which European city you are in by how the motorists treat pedestrians. In London, motorists generally stop for you. In Rome, they weave around you at disconcertingly high speeds. In Paris, they change direction, accelerate, and aim at you, seeing it as some kind of competitive sport.

2   I'd once bet Tom a beer that the magnificent beard sported by the previous Archbishop of Canterbury had been a fake. Tom had met Rowan Williams at a literary festival and had conclusively proved it was real, winning the bet along with a police caution and a restraining order.

3   A writer's euphemism for "I looked it up on Google".

atheist Richard Dawkins, and represented, in their words, an attempt to provide a "peaceful and upbeat" message about atheism. The advertisements promoted a website where those who browsed could while away their journey on the number 137 bus to Battersea reading about the joys of life without belief in a god.

The atheist bus is a good place to begin our journey, because it illustrates two reasons why this book exists. First, because the slogan, despite its friendly pink letters, is a perfect example of a really bad argument. An argument so bad, so disastrous, in fact, that one has to wonder what its sponsors were thinking. More on that in a moment. But, second, it illustrates how quickly bad arguments can disseminate, spreading like an infestation of Japanese knotweed into popular culture. For while many critics – including many *atheist* critics[4] – were quick to point out the flaws in "There's Probably No God. Now Stop Worrying and Enjoy Your Life", it has nevertheless continued to pop up on the sides of buses not just in London but also around the world.

The bus advertisement typifies what's come to be termed the "New Atheism", a phrase coined back in 2006 by *Wired* magazine to describe the group of media-savvy atheists – men such as Richard Dawkins, Sam Harris, Daniel Dennett, and the late Christopher Hitchens – whose books attacking religion in general and Christianity in particular have sold by the truckload.[5] What's new about the "New Atheism"? As many have pointed out, not so much its *arguments*, which tend to be old ones, as its

---

4   See e.g. Julian Baggini, "Yes, life without God can be bleak. Atheism is about facing up to that", *The Guardian*, 9 March 2012 (http://www.theguardian.com/commentisfree/2012/mar/09/life-without-god-bleak-atheism).

5   See the article by Gary Wolf, "The Church of the Non-Believers", *Wired* magazine, November 2006 (http://www.wired.com/wired/archive/14.11/atheism.html). There's also a good survey in Vox Day, *The Irrational Atheist: Dissecting the Unholy Trinity of Dawkins, Harris, and Hitchens*, Dallas, TX: BenBella Books, 2008, pp. 5–26.

tone – which is one of apoplectic anger. Why the anger? Well, I suspect partly because God was supposed to have disappeared a long time ago, as the Great Secular Enlightenment trundled inexorably onward. As far back as 1966, *Time* magazine could slap a question like "Is God Dead?" on the cover (with the strong implication that the answer was "Yes"). Today, however, religion is alive and well and shows little sign of disappearing.[6] The failure of God to roll over and die on cue has led to the denial, disappointment, and anger that can be seen underpinning much of today's more popular form of atheism.

And, my word, has the New Atheism become a popular movement. Richard Dawkins's book *The God Delusion* alone has sold several million copies.[7] Atheism has gained a voice and a confidence, and that's fine – in the past, it was tough to be an atheist, when most societies were overwhelmingly religious. Recently, however, there's been a cultural volte-face in many Western countries, with atheism now seen as the default position. Many people assume that atheism is, indeed, the *only* position for somebody who wishes to be considered educated, sophisticated, urbane, and rational. This is precisely the way the media often treats the issue too: atheism is portrayed as scientific, contemporary, and for those with brains, whereas religion is characterized as stuffy, outmoded, and irrational, something for old ladies or fuddy-duddies.[8]

But there's a problem. Well, several problems. Chief among

---

6   See section six of Rodney Stark, *The Triumph of Christianity: How the Jesus Movement Became The World's Largest Religion*, New York: HarperOne, 2011.

7   Largely helped, at least in North America, by his British accent. As an Englishman living in Canada, I have lost count of how many people have remarked to me after lectures, "You could have said *anything* in that accent and I would have been impressed." They always look crestfallen when I point out that this is not a compliment.

8   It also used to be the case that religious believers were associated with poor fashion sense, but several of the New Atheists have taken admirable steps toward redressing the balance in that regard.

them is this: that much of contemporary atheism thrives on poor arguments and cheap sound bites, advancing claims that simply don't stand up to scrutiny. Like a cheaply made cardigan, they're full of loose threads that, if tugged firmly, quickly begin to unravel. Let me demonstrate what I mean by returning to that notorious bus advertisement, "There's Probably No God. Now Stop Worrying and Enjoy Your Life". Let's ask a few critical questions about that claim for a moment. What's wrong with it? Well, one might begin by noting the preachy, condescending, and hectoring tone.[9] I've known many atheists over the years whose chief beef with religion has been that they can't escape it. If it's not televangelists with perfect teeth, it's church billboards with dodgy graphic design or giant advertising hoardings warning of hellfire and damnation. "You religious types insist on preaching at us" is the complaint. Well, now the boot is very much on the other foot and the New Atheism is zealously evangelistic, not merely content with denying deities but offering health benefits at the same time (No worries! Enjoyment! Good hair!).

But there's a deeper problem, too. For atheists like Richard Dawkins, God does not exist, right? That, after all, is what the very term "a-theist" means. Of course, there's a myriad of other things that don't exist: fairies, unicorns, the Flying Spaghetti Monster, successful England soccer squads.[10] But here's my question: what's the connection between the non-existence of something and any *effect*, emotional or otherwise? There probably aren't any unicorns, so cheer up. The Flying Spaghetti Monster is just a secular parody, so take heart. There's no God, so quit worrying.

9   Which, when I first saw it, struck me as sounding a bit like a slightly grumpy elderly uncle: "There's probably no dessert, young man, so stop dawdling and eat up your sprouts."
10   The English specialize in inventing sports, and then getting beaten by the rest of the world at them. I like to think this displays not so much a lack of sporting prowess as modesty; we like to give other nations a chance.

How, precisely, does that work? Somebody once remarked that a nonsensical statement doesn't become coherent simply because you insert the term "God" into it, so let's illustrate the problem by rewording the atheist bus slogan for a moment:

There's Probably No Loch Ness Monster. So Stop Worrying and Enjoy Your Life.

Imagine, for a moment, that you're down on your luck. Life has dealt you a series of terrible hands and nothing seems to be going your way. You've recently lost your job. Your wife has just left you and taken the kids with her.[11] This very morning, a letter from your bank has arrived, declaring you bankrupt. The doctor's surgery has just rung to inform you that those worrying headaches are actually Creutzfeldt-Jakob disease. Oh, and you're a Bradford City FC fan.[12] Life really sucks. Have no fear, however. Put all that aside. Fret no more. For there is hope. There is an end to all worries. "There *is*?" I hear you cry, wiping back the tears. Yes, there is. Because (are you ready for this?) *the Loch Ness Monster doesn't exist.* Never mind the fact that you may be jobless, loveless, penniless, and hopeless, doesn't it warm the cockles of your heart to know that holidaymakers in Scotland can munch their sandwiches by Urquhart Castle and paddle their feet in Loch Ness, safe in the certain knowledge that no monster from the Jurassic era will rear up from the deep and drag them off to a watery grave. So, are you feeling better now? No, probably not.

So the first half of the claim – no God, no worry – fails spectacularly. The second half doesn't fare much better either:

11   If you're a parent of teenagers, feel free to reword this to "*left* the kids with you".
12   These cultural references are tough, aren't they? For Canadians, think of the Toronto Maple Leafs, or, for Americans, think of the Chicago Cubs. I've concluded that the only reason people follow teams like these is either that misery loves company, or that masochism never entirely goes out of fashion.

"Enjoy your life." What could be wrong with that, unless you're one of those masochistic religious types who prefer guilt to glee? Well, Francis Spufford nails this one perfectly:

> I'm sorry – *enjoy* your life? Enjoy your *life*? I'm not making some kind of neo-puritan objection to enjoyment. Enjoyment is lovely. Enjoyment is great. The more enjoyment the better. But enjoyment is *one emotion*. The only things in the world that are designed to elicit enjoyment and only enjoyment are products, and your life is not a product ... To say that life is to be enjoyed (just enjoyed) is like saying that mountains should have only summits, or that all colours should be purple, or that all plays should be by Shakespeare. This really is a bizarre category error.[13]

In other words, there is considerably more to life than just enjoyment. Indeed, the full gamut of human emotions spans the alphabet. To be fully, authentically human is to have experienced anger, boredom, compassion, delight, expectation, fear, guilt, hope, insecurity, joy, kindness, love, malice, nonchalance, obligation, peace, queasiness, relief, sensuality, thankfulness, uneasiness, vulnerability, wistfulness, yearning, and zealousness.[14] Given all this, why does the atheist bus advertisement zero in on "enjoyment"? Now obviously I'm not privy to the interior mental state of those who penned the slogan, but I do wonder if it's a symptom of a more general trend in our culture – one that says that the purpose of human life is simply to be happy, to flit merrily from one experience to

---

13   Francis Spufford, *Unapologetic: Why, Despite Everything, Christianity Can Still Make Surprising Emotional Sense*, London: Faber & Faber, 2013, p. 8.

14   I tried hard to find a feeling beginning with "x", I really did, but the best I could come up with was "xenophobic". It staggers me there aren't more emotions beginning with "x". I blame the French; that usually works.

another in an effervescence of ecstatic enjoyment. Product after product is sold to us this way: buy *this* coffee, take *that* holiday, wear *this* shade of lip gloss, and you'll be successful, popular, and joyful. The atheist bus is simply riding the cultural wave – think like *this*, it says, and you'll be happy.

But what if you're *not* happy? What if you're like my earlier example – jobless, friendless, penniless, and hopeless? What if you're at a point in your life where all is smelling not of roses, but rather suspiciously like a sewage farm on a hot afternoon? Indeed, half the world's population lives on less than $2.50 a day and that amount is not going to keep you in lattes, lipstick or trips to Lanzarote, which means that, if the advertisers are correct about where enjoyment is located, you're in trouble, so you'd better pull yourself together. I stress *you*, second person singular, had better pull yourself together, because, if the atheist bus slogan is right and there is no God, there's nobody out *there* who is ultimately going to help with any pulling. You're alone in a universe that cares as little about you (and your enjoyment) as it does about the fate of the amoeba, the ant or the aardvark. There's no hope, there's no justice, and there's certainly nothing inherently wrong with poverty, incidentally, so quit protesting. Life favours the winners; some get the breaks, and others get the sticky end of the stick. Still others get to make millions selling books on atheism,[15] enough for a lifetime of lattes. Enjoy your life? Nice work if you can get it.

⌘

---

15   Or by charging people $100,000 to have a private breakfast with you: see Andrew Brown, "The bizarre – and costly – cult of Richard Dawkins", *The Spectator*, 16 August 2014 (available online at http://www.spectator.co.uk/features/9286682/the-bizarre-and-costly-cult-of-richard-dawkins/).

The atheist bus advertisement illustrates the danger not just of poor arguments, but especially of *argument by sound bite*. It's easy to sloganize lazily, to try to reduce complex arguments to something that fits on the side of a bus or sounds good on Twitter, but in so doing you usually lose nuance and depth. In fact, it's worse than that: the temptation to sloganize can result in arguments that are not merely wrong but are utterly bizarre and have some terrible consequences when you turn them around. Let me further illustrate what I mean with an example from one of New Atheism's founding fathers, Richard Dawkins. His publishing success has helped to make atheism hip and cool again but while he has done terrifically well in print, his other cultural forays have not always been entirely successful. For instance, his attempt at a movie, *The Unbelievers*, bombed at the box office, while his faux pas on social media have become somewhat legendary.[16] The danger of being a celebrity is that fame can lure you into believing that every fluttering thought should be served up raw to the masses. It's awfully easy, for example, to tap out something like this quickly on one's smartphone:

> Stalin, Hitler and Saddam Hussein were evil, murdering dictators. All had moustaches. Therefore moustaches are evil.[17]

I imagine your reaction on reading that is to think "Huh?" *Sans* context, it does look a little baffling. Alas, I'm not entirely sure

---

16   See Brendan O'Neill, "Let the fate of Richard Dawkins be a lesson to you all – Twitter brings out the worst in humankind", *The Telegraph*, 13 March 2014 (online at http://blogs.telegraph.co.uk/news/brendanoneill2/100263460/let-the-fate-of-richard-dawkins-be-a-lesson-to-you-all-twitter-brings-out-the-worst-in-humankind/).

17   Richard Dawkins (@RichardDawkins), 2 March 2014, 5:14 p.m., https://twitter.com/RichardDawkins/status/440233751965364224.

that adding context helps, but here goes. What Dawkins was trying to do via this tweet was to respond to his critics who have said that it's a little troubling to try to label religion as the "root of all evil",[18] given the many *atheist* mass murderers who litter the historical record. If you're trying to advance the claim that religion is *bad* and atheism is *good*, the likes of Saddam Hussein, Joseph Stalin, Pol Pot, and Mao Zedong are somewhat troubling, slugs on the otherwise pristine lettuce of atheism.[19] It's one thing to point out the evils of religion (the Crusades and the Spanish Inquisition being among the favourite whipping boys), but what about atheism's own chequered history? Stalin was responsible for the deaths of some 20 million people, while the death toll for Mao's regime is at least double that. These were avowed atheists, so what is the zealous young secularist to do? Enter Richard Dawkins's tweet, one that he probably thought a brilliant rhetorical move. Sure, all of those mass-murdering psychotic despots were atheists, but that's got nothing to do with their villainous genocidal tendencies. Yes, they had *atheism* in common, but they also had *moustaches* in common. Perhaps it was their facial hair, not their secular air, that led to their causing the deaths of tens of millions of people.

Does that work? In a word, "no". Listen to me very carefully here. I have no intention, none whatsoever, of laying

---

18   That was the title of Dawkins's 2006 TV series that later got expanded into *The God Delusion*. Personally, I always thought that the root of all evil was folk music.

19   Hitler is a somewhat unique case. Christians and atheist apologists are both occasionally guilty of suggesting Hitler was a card-carrying member of the opposite side, but the truth is that Hitler seems to have cobbled together a unique set of beliefs, drawn from religion and science and mashed up to produce a toxic nationalistic myth. When you read the history of the Third Reich, what you discover is that nobody comes off well. Too many Christians and atheists stood by and did nothing, while there were also brave men and women of all beliefs who took a stand. One famous Christian example is the German pastor Dietrich Bonhoeffer, whose stance against the Third Reich ultimately led to his death. See Eric Metaxas, *Bonhoeffer: Pastor, Martyr, Prophet, Spy*, Nashville, TN: Thomas Nelson, 2010.

the blame for what these men and others like them did at the feet of my atheist friends. But my point is this: we can read the writings of brutal tyrants such as these and discover what they themselves said about their motivations. For example, Stalin once stated: "You know, they are fooling us, there is no God ... all this talk about God is sheer nonsense." But Stalin was not content with mere words; he also acted on them. In 1925, he actively encouraged the founding of the League of Militant Atheists, which for over twenty years acted out its slogan, "The Struggle Against Religion is a Struggle for Socialism". It began with popular campaigns in the media against religion, aiming to persuade citizens that religion was irrational and toxic. But soon things became considerably more violent:

> Churches were closed or destroyed, often by dynamiting; priests were imprisoned, exiled or executed. On the eve of the Second World War there were only 6,376 clergy remaining in the Russian Orthodox Church, compared with the pre-revolutionary figure of 66,140. One dreadful day, 17 February 1938, saw the execution of 55 priests. In 1917 there were 39,530 churches in Russia; by 1940, only 950 remained functional.[20]

Similar stories could be told of Pol Pot or Mao Zedong, or numerous other atheistic dictators. When I lived in Europe, I frequently travelled and taught in former communist countries such as Hungary and Romania and heard story after story of the violence that had been endemic before the Iron Curtain fell in 1989. One woman in Bucharest told me how she'd missed out on large amounts of education as a child, because

---

20 Alister McGrath, *Why God Won't Go Away: Engaging with the New Atheism*, London: SPCK, 2011, p. 51; see also Roger Moorhouse, *The Devils' Alliance: Hitler's Pact with Stalin*, 1939–1941, London: Bodley Head, 2014.

her parents were religious. They'd been given a stark choice by the communist authorities: give up your faith, or give up your child's education.

Here's the problem, then, for Dawkins's attempt to claim that the atheism of Stalin is unimportant. When we look at Stalin's actions, his atheism seems entirely *central*, quite frankly. When he came to power, Stalin did not ban razor blades and announce a pogrom against barbers, but he did burn churches and synagogues and have thousands of religious leaders arrested, tortured, and executed. Yet if Dawkins is right, we can ignore all of this. We can lay aside what Stalin did and said – ignore *Stalin's very own reasons* – and instead offer a random explanation of our own making, one that suits our own purposes. Look, Stalin had a moustache![21] Don't look at his atheism; look at his facial hair!

The problem is that, like all terrible arguments, this cuts both ways.[22] Let me illustrate what I mean by considering Dawkins himself. Why do you suppose that he wrote his atheist manifesto, *The God Delusion*? If you read the preface of the book, he claims that it was to advance atheism, to persuade people to abandon religious faith, and to raise "atheist pride". But, of course, those are *his* explanations and, as Dawkins helpfully reminded us with Stalin, you can't simply take a person's own words and assume they are, well, gospel. So what should we do? Well, perhaps we should, à la Stalin's moustache, settle on

---

21 In the light of Dawkins's tweet, it's curious to observe that Pol Pot and Mao Zedong actually appear to have spent most of their life clean-shaven. Either Dawkins is privy to some collection of antique photographs unbeknown to historians, or it's worse than we thought: Pol Pot and Mao Zedong knew their moustaches would betray them as potential mass murderers, so they carefully bleached their facial hair so fine that it couldn't be seen. Am I the only one who thinks that *Invisible Killer Moustaches* sounds like an amazing title for a Hollywood blockbuster?

22 Unlike Stalin's razor.

something purely at random to explain *The God Delusion* – perhaps Dawkins's predilection for garishly coloured neckties, or his fondness for prawn cocktail.[23] However, that would be woefully simplistic. We can be *way* more scientific than that. Listen to these words from another atheist writer, the philosopher Patricia Churchland:

> Boiled down to the essentials, a nervous system enables the organism to succeed at four things: feeding, fleeing, fighting and reproducing ... Truth, whatever that is, definitely takes the hindmost.[24]

In this astonishingly bleak passage, Churchland is trying to argue that human beings are just like any other animal, driven by our basest, most primal instincts to feed, fight, flee or reproduce. Our cherished belief that we are concerned with truth or meaning is just an illusion, a trick played on us by our DNA in order to get us to cooperate.[25] Impressed? You should be; after all, this is Science™. Well, actually it isn't; it's philosophy, wearing a false nose and rubber ears and *masquerading* as science. But, nevertheless, let's apply Churchland's four options to the vexed question of why Dawkins wrote *The God Delusion*. Perchance he wrote it for reasons of *feeding*. After all, the book has presumably funded numerous hearty dinners at places like Gee's in Oxford[26]; indeed, the sales figures suggest that Dawkins won't be found shopping for groceries at Lidl for some time to

---

23   He has the shellfish gene.
24   Patricia Churchland, "Epistemology in the Age of Neuroscience", *Journal of Philosophy* 84.10 , 1987, pp. 544–553, citing 548.
25   Of course, that raises an excellent question: if human beings are unconcerned with truth, why did Churchland bother typing that sentence? Or any sentence? Why go through the pretence of arguing for anything? If she were consistent, Churchland ought to quit teaching, take up jogging and kick-boxing, and spend any remaining free time munching cheeseburgers and seducing undergraduates.
26   Try the sea bass.

come. Alternatively, perhaps the book was written for purposes of *fleeing*. Should Dawkins be startled by a bunch of militant Mennonites in a darkened Oxford alley, he can fling it at them, yell "Permian extinction", and, while they're thumbing through the extensive index,[27] he will have time to scarper. The third of Churchland's options, *fighting*, is a little harder to see, but it occurs to me that *The God Delusion* is a brick of a book, so one might certainly wield the hardback edition quite usefully in a pub brawl. And, finally, what about *reproducing*? Well, one can easily imagine how "I'm a famous author, don't you know?" could open many a hotel-room door at the kind of secular conferences frequented by pretty young sceptics. In short, we can ignore every single one of Dawkins's protestations that he wrote *The God Delusion* to advance atheism and come up with our own reasons. What goes for Stalin goes for Dawkins. Mous-*touché*, one might very well say.

You will be very relieved to learn that all of the above is in jest. But there is a serious point, a *very* serious point, and it's this: the thing about bad arguments, about sound bites without substance, is that they are extremely vulnerable to satire. They may sound clever, bright, and shiny when you first hear them, especially if they are accompanied by an Oxford accent or the jangle of PhDs and titles. But stick a pin in them and they deflate quite rapidly.

So how can we learn to spot which arguments are good ones and which are not? One of the tests is to see what happens when one transfers an argument to a different setting. This is what we have just demonstrated with "There's Probably No God. Now Stop Worrying and Enjoy Your Life" and "Moustaches Are More Dangerous Than Atheism". When one pokes at them a

---

27 Unless they have the e-book edition with them and can simply hit "Search", in which case he's basically toast.

bit – and especially when one tries applying them to something else – one quickly sees the flaws. They are both examples of not just weak arguments, but extremely bad arguments. Arguments so terrible, in fact, that you wonder what possessed people to place them on buses, reproduce them in print, or tweet them to a million hapless followers. When you see such things in the media, or hear them on the lips of friends, don't be afraid to ask a few questions, tug at loose threads, to gently expose them for what they are.

⌘

One last thought. I come at this discussion as a *Christian* philosopher, but I have been struck by how many of my *atheist* friends are deeply embarrassed by these terrible sceptical arguments.[28] I have lost count of how many times I have quoted Richard Dawkins at atheist friends only to have them roll their eyes, eject steam from both ears, and retort, "Please don't assume we're all like him" or "I won't wave Fred Phelps at you if you don't pin the New Atheists on me". And that's a very fair point, although I do wish a few more of my atheist friends would speak out, so that the media and the Twitter crowd would realize that there are more thoughtful secularists out there.

And so the aim of this book is simple: to clear away some of the weeds of bad arguments so that a more sensible dialogue can be had. Because here's the thing: the "God Question" is arguably the most important question that anybody can think about. Whether or not God exists is not a mere intellectual curiosity, up there with "What's the ten trillionth digit of Pi?" or "Did Newton invent the cat flap?", but a question that has

---

28   See e.g. Theodore Dalrymple, "What the New Atheists Don't See", *City Journal* 17.4, 2007 (online at http://www.city-journal.org/html/17_4_oh_to_be.html).

implications for every area of our lives, not least because it is directly tied to the question of meaning: is there something that we are meant to *be*, or is a life spent playing computer games and eating pizza as valid as one spent fighting poverty or serving the cause of justice?

At the beginning of *The God Delusion*, Richard Dawkins is very honest about the chief aim of his own book:

> If this book works as intended, religious readers who open it will be atheists when they put it down. What presumptuous optimism! Of course, dyed-in-the-wool faith-heads are immune to argument, their resistance built up over years of childhood indoctrination using methods that took centuries to mature.[29]

That's a clever paragraph, when you think about it. If you read Dawkins's book and *don't* become an atheist, it's not that the arguments are as suspect as a $50 Rolex from Tooting Market but because you're an ignorant brainwashed cretin, your head so full of woolly thinking that there's no room for the fresh winds of Reason™ to waft through. My aims for *this* book are a little more modest (and, I trust, a little more optimistic) than those of Dawkins. If you come to this book as an atheist, my hope is simply that you will at least commit to being a *thought-through* atheist – perhaps a doubter, rather than a sceptic; somebody who is willing to think deeply and think well. (It has been remarked that the difference between a doubter and a sceptic is that a doubter is somebody who hopes there *might* be an answer; a sceptic hopes that there *isn't*). Abandoning bad

---

29   Richard Dawkins, *The God Delusion*, London: Transworld, 2006, p. 28; a similar rhetorically sophomoric strategy is pursued by Peter Boghossian, *A Manual for Creating Atheists*, Durham, NC: Pitchstone Publishing, 2013, p. 51, who suggests that if you disagree with him, it's not because his arguments are poor, but because you're brain-damaged.

arguments is a great way to begin.

Conversely, if you come to this book as a religious believer, my hope is that it will encourage you not to be afraid of some of the atheist sound bites that are frequently hurled like brickbats from various directions in our culture. If you can learn to laugh at bad arguments and their flaws, their mystical power evaporates and you can see them for the paper tigers that they are. I also hope that I might encourage you to see past the ranting of the New Atheists to recognize that there are thousands of far more open-minded atheists out there, people who are friendly, good-humoured, and open to discussion. What the world needs more than ever is a reasonable dialogue between those who believe in God and those who have questions or doubts (however deeply held), not a clash of fundamentalisms.

So, wherever you stand as you start this book – atheist or agnostic, seeker or sceptic, doubter or disciple – I hope that we can *all* agree that, when it comes to the big questions of life, we need more than sound bites. Let's aim instead for a grown-up, proper conversation about the things that matter the most and leave the buses to the fundamentalists.

For Further Reading

Vox Day, *The Irrational Atheist: Dissecting the Unholy Trinity of Dawkins, Harris, and Hitchens* (Dallas, TX: BenBella Books, 2008)

John Lennox, *Gunning for God: Why the New Atheists are Missing the Target* (Oxford: Lion, 2011)

Alister McGrath, *Why God Won't Go Away: Engaging with the New Atheism* (London: SPCK, 2011)

Francis Spufford, *Unapologetic: Why, Despite Everything, Christianity Can Still Make Surprising Emotional Sense* (London: Faber & Faber, 2013)

2

The Scandinavian Sceptic

(or: Why Atheism Really is a Belief System)

"I don't believe that Sweden exists!" my friend suddenly announced from across the coffee-shop table. "There! I've finally said it." He took a long sip of espresso and stared fiercely at me, clearly daring me to respond. I paused for a moment to think, my cinnamon roll halfway to my mouth as I digested what he'd just said.

"Pardon?"

"Sweden doesn't exist. I am a Scandinavian scoffer, a Nordic nullifidian, a Sverigeinian[30] sceptic ..."

"And clearly the possessor of *quite* some thesaurus. But, seriously, you don't believe in Sweden?"

"That's right. It's obvious when you think about it: Sweden is just a political conspiracy, invented to motivate other European citizens to work harder. All that talk of the best healthcare system, the highest standard of living, tall, svelte, and beautiful

---

30   That really should be a word.

people.[31] Come on, it sounds more and more like a myth every time you hear it. But I'm not fooled. I do not believe in Sweden."

I stared at my friend silently, allowing the sounds of the coffee shop to drift over us for a few seconds while I pondered. In the background, the radio began playing "Dancing Queen" by ABBA.

"You're insane," I said. "What do you mean, you don't believe in Sweden? That's *ridiculous*. If Sweden doesn't exist, how do you explain IKEA furniture, or the Swedish Chef on *The Muppet Show*, or what glues Norway to Finland. That's a staggering claim! What's your evidence?"

"Evidence?" my friend asked.

"Yes, *evidence*. You surely have more than just a hunch and a bunch of prejudices, and must have some pretty impressive evidence for your belief. I realize that Sweden has only 9.5 million inhabitants and more moose than men, but you can't simply deny outright that it exists."

"Ah," said my friend, knowingly, "I see your problem."

"*My* problem?"

"Yes, *your* problem. In fact, your *confusion*. You think that my denial of Sweden is an actual claim of some kind, that it's a belief. But it isn't. It's a *non*-belief. There's nothing I need to explain – rather, I'm talking about something I *lack*, namely a belief in Sweden, so I don't need to give any evidence for it."

"Come again?" I said.

"Yes," he continued, warming to his theme, "I don't have to provide evidence for my non-belief in Atlantis, El Dorado, Shangri-La or the Customer Support Department at American

---

31   I have often travelled in the Nordic countries and being blond-haired and blue-eyed am sometimes mistaken for a Swede. At least when sitting down. Once I stand up and my full height of five foot eight is revealed, the illusion is quickly dispelled. Then I announce that I'm a Bonsai Viking.

Airlines, and nor need I for my non-belief in Sweden. I'm not making a claim of *any* kind – in fact, quite the opposite: I'm claiming *nothing*. I'm merely rejecting one of your beliefs, your belief in Sweden. Now, quit arguing and pass me another slice of Prinsesstårta."

⌘

While that dialogue was, unsurprisingly, entirely fictional, the response from my friend concerning the reasons (or rather the absence thereof) for his doubts about Sweden have some real-world parallels, especially in the way that some atheists like to describe their non-belief in God. The argument goes this way: atheism is a *disbelief* in God, and therefore one does not need to give reasons for it. The idea lying behind this is that atheism is purely negative, the mere *absence* of belief, and it is only *positive* beliefs for which we need to provide reasons. For instance, should I claim that my bathtub is presently occupied by two magnificent hippos who are at this very moment engaged in a hearty duet of "Mud, Mud, Glorious Mud!" (one singing, one accompanying on the kazoo), then of course I can be asked to provide evidence. On the other hand, should I announce: "My bathroom is entirely devoid of any examples of *hippopotamus amphibius*", I need not go any further to justify myself.

So *is* atheism purely the *absence* of belief, a wholly negative claim? Well, certainly many atheists seem to think so. For example, listen to the late New Atheist Christopher Hitchens:

Our belief is not a belief.[32]

---

32   Christopher Hitchens, *God is Not Great*, London: Atlantic Books, 2007, p. 5.

That's a mental tongue-twister if ever I saw one. Here's another example, this time from one of the evangelistic young atheists who hover around my Twitter feed like moths around a hurricane lamp:

> Atheism isn't a claim. It's just non-belief in the claim "There is a god".

I have lost track of how many times I have heard variations of this. Rhetorically, it's a smart move: if atheism is simply a negative claim, the mere *absence* of belief, then presumably atheists can sit there and throw stones at everybody else's beliefs, while not having to bother justifying their own. Like my friend in the coffee shop, they can innocently deny they are claiming *anything*, and refuse to give any reasons. However, like many secular sound bites, the idea that atheism is a non-belief is riddled with as many holes as a Swiss cheese. Let's explore some of the chief difficulties with the idea.

The first problem is that the statement "Atheism is just non-belief in God" *proves too much*. What do I mean? Well, if this claim is true, consider what it entails. It would mean, for instance, that my cat is an atheist, because she does not believe in God.[33] Likewise potatoes, the colour green, Richard Dawkins's left foot, and small rocks are all atheists because they, too, do not possess a belief in a deity of any kind. Like the IKEA food hall, something here smells a bit fishy. When I've mentioned this to atheist friends, the usual response is: "But a potato can't believe *anything*!" To which I always reply: "So you're now saying that atheism is the lack of belief in God by a creature

---

33   I sometimes suspect that cats believe that they *are* God, but that's another story entirely. If you want to explore this, you might start with Terry Pratchett and Gray Jolliffe's *The Unadulterated Cat: A Campaign for Real Cats*, London: Vista, 1992.

that has the ability to form beliefs?" You see that is a different claim entirely. Why? Because it's a *positive* claim. My atheist friend is now claiming that she believes that the external world *really* exists, that we are not simply brains in a jar, our thoughts and experiences manipulated like those of the humans in *The Matrix* movies. Furthermore, she is claiming that other minds exist, that it is possible for the human brain to form beliefs, and that our thinking is more or less reliable.[34]

Suddenly, what looked to be a simple, innocent statement of non-belief ("I don't believe in God!") has suddenly morphed into not just one but a whole series of *positive claims*, popping up like mushrooms after a rainstorm. And this is hugely significant, because I have not yet encountered an atheist who believes that *positive* claims do not need to be argued for; indeed, atheists are fond of crying "Evidence! Evidence!" when confronted with a religious believer. Now sauce for the goose is definitely sauce for the oven-ready chicken, and thus the atheist is likewise required to give *evidence* for each of the philosophical positions they are encamped on. If they are not willing to do the hard thinking that this involves, well then, they can take their place along with the cat, the rock, and the potato. Oh, and Richard Dawkins's foot, to boot.

However, it gets worse. Think back to our Scandinavian sceptic and his idea that the claim "Sweden doesn't exist" is not a belief. If he is correct and it is not a belief, then, sure, I guess he doesn't need to defend it. But, at the same time, if he is correct then something else follows too: namely that his statement cannot be true *or* false. Like many philosophical ideas, this can take a moment to get your head around, but when you grasp

---

34   If we wished to display further pedantry, we might also point out that our atheist friend also needs to believe that language can convey meaning. In other words, when she says: "I am an atheist", she clearly believes she is saying *something*. The question of precisely what is one that linguists and philosophers have argued about for centuries.

it, it's obvious. The problem is that only *beliefs* or *claims* can be true or false. For example, it makes perfect sense to ask whether a statement such as "It is raining today" or "The Maple Leafs lost the hockey again" are true.[35] Those are claims, they are beliefs, and they have what philosophers call a "truth value". They are either true or false. On the other hand, it is utterly meaningless to ask whether the colour blue, a small off-duty Slovakian traffic warden, or Richard Dawkins's left foot is "true". That would be a bizarre category error. These things are not claims or beliefs and thus do not possess any kind of truth value. They simply are.

So what about atheism? Well, as far as I can make out, I *think* my atheist friends are claiming that their belief is true; that they really, really believe it to be *true* that there is no God. Well, if that's the case, then it makes atheism a positive claim and claims must be defended, evidence martialled, and reasons given. Otherwise, if atheism is *not* a claim, it cannot be true or false. It simply *is*, and to say "I am an atheist" is up there with saying "Wibble, wibble, wibble".[36] If my atheist friends wish to join the conversation sensibly – and I believe that atheism deserves its seat at the table of discussion as much as any other world view – then they must recognize their belief for what it is and engage accordingly.

"Hang on, though! What about the hippopotamus?" I hear some readers cry.

"The hippopotamus?"

"Yes, the hippopotamus. If what you say is true, then surely announcing 'There is no hippopotamus in the bathroom'

---

35   Many Canadians, especially Torontonians, suspect that the statement "The Maple Leafs lost the hockey again" is *necessarily* true.
36   Fans of the British TV sitcom *Blackadder* know where this can end, especially if said while wearing your underpants on your head and with a pencil stuffed up each nostril.

*is also a positive belief, and thus I need to defend it. Likewise
my lack of belief in the Tooth Fairy, Bigfoot, the Yeti, and James
Blunt's singing ability. Doesn't all this get extremely tiring, if not
practically impossible?"*

Good point. Does all that I have said mean I have to be
willing to trot out mountains of evidence whenever I admit I
disbelieve in gigantic bathroom-dwelling mammals? Well, that
depends. Whereas I don't spend much of my day thinking about
the hippopotami-free zone in which I perform my morning
ablutions, if I daily tweeted: "There is no hippo" or if I were
to start self-defining as an "ahippopotamusian", people would
be justified in asking me "Why?", "What gives?", or possibly
"Would you like the number of my therapist?" I think we all
instinctively know there is a definite difference between *active*
beliefs and *passive* beliefs. There are a near-infinite number
of things I passively don't believe in, if you were to press me:
everything from floating celestial teapots to unicycling unicorns.
But I have never, not once, felt the need to write *The Invisible
Floating Teapot Behind Jupiter Delusion*. On the other hand,
there are plenty of things I *actively* disbelieve: for example, I do
not believe that George Mallory and Andrew Irvine made it to
the summit of Everest in June 1924, beating Edmund Hillary
and Tenzing Norgay by some thirty years. I have read most of
the literature and the arguments on both sides, so I can give you
reasons for my non-belief. For our *active* non-beliefs, disbeliefs
that consume our time and energy, for those, yes, we *do* need
to give reasons.

But for other, lesser, non-beliefs, we don't, and thus we can
safely dismiss protestations about bathroom hippos and the
Tooth Fairy quite easily. Why? Because those non-beliefs don't
lead to *action*. Think about this for a moment: it is only actual,

existent things that cause anything. For example, dropping a sledgehammer on your foot *causes* pain. Turning the ignition key on your Toyota *causes* the engine to start. Touching the screen of your iPod *causes* an ABBA track to play through your headphones and your eardrums to ache. But non-existent sledgehammers, non-existent keys or non-existent iPods cause *nothing at all*. Now when it comes to beliefs, much the same applies. Non-belief in hippos in the bathroom has never *caused* anything. Nor does non-belief in the Tooth Fairy (although it might conceivably *prevent* actions, such as not putting your teeth under the pillow when they fall out).[37] It seems that, for something to *cause* an action, it has to be a positive belief, an actual claim.

So what about atheism? Well, it doesn't take a lot of thought to realize that atheism causes all manner of actions. For a non-belief, it leads a pretty busy and exciting life. For example, many Internet-dwelling atheists spend hundreds of hours reading sceptical websites, editing Wikipedia articles, writing angry blogs, frequenting atheist discussion forums, and posting snarky anti-religious remarks on Twitter. These look very much like actions to me. Actions, I presume, *caused* by their atheism. The same applies offline too. I know many atheists who attend conferences, buy T-shirts with atheist slogans, or fasten amusing atheist bumper stickers to their Hondas. Some, like Richard Dawkins, write books. Now, there's a puzzler. Why *did* Richard Dawkins write *The God Delusion*? We've asked that question before, but now we can come at it from a different

---

37 I had a childhood friend who was terrified of the monsters under the bed, so he did the sensible thing and slept with his head under the pillow. All was well and good until somebody helpfully warned him that, if did that, he risked the Tooth Fairy coming past and leaving him nothing but gums. On such childhood hang-ups the entire edifice of psychotherapy is erected.

angle. What was it that drove him to pour endless hours into typing, drafting, editing, and refining? Presumably, it was his atheism. Likewise, it was atheism that led many enthusiastic young sceptics to rush out and buy it, causing, if not much rejoicing in heaven, certainly much celebration in the North Oxford branch of whomever Dawkins banks with. For a non-belief, a non-thing, atheism looks extraordinarily lively, and thus we need to be a little suspicious of anybody who tells us that atheism is nothing at all.

⌘

Another hallmark of an actual belief is that is has *entailments*, consequences that follow from it. If I rush out of my bathroom, stark naked, à la Archimedes, yelling "Eureka!"[38] and "There is *no* hippopotamus!" nothing much follows (except possibly a police caution and a recommendation to don a dressing gown next time). On the other hand, other non-beliefs have considerable consequences. For instance, the denial that Sweden exists brings with it the need to find a new source of cheap pine furniture, meatballs, and gravad lax. It also has some pretty drastic consequences for geography, requiring a complete redrawing of the map of Northern Europe, as well as having major implications for the writers of 1970s tribute musicals.[39]

So, if a sign of a *positive* belief is that it has actual entailments, real consequences in the real world, what about atheism? Does anything follow from denying that God exists? One of the most famous atheists of the last 200 years, Friedrich Nietzsche, certainly thought so. He wrote:

---

38   I believe Archimedes' neighbours responded to his cry of "Eureka!" with "You don't smell too good either".

39   The comedian Bill Bailey once described listening to *Mamma Mia* as like being smacked around the head by a piece of IKEA furniture: it hurts, but you've got to admire the craftsmanship.

> When one gives up the Christian faith, one pulls the
> right to Christian morality out from under one's feet.
> This morality is by no means self-evident ... Christianity
> is a system, a whole view of things thought out together.
> By breaking one main concept out of it, the faith in God,
> one breaks the whole: nothing necessary remains in
> one's hands.[40]

Nietzsche is pointing out that just as if you dynamite the foundations of your home, the walls and roof will collapse and you'll be left with so much rubble, so too with God. Many things stand upon belief in God, such as the idea that human beings have intrinsic value. Ethics, law, and human rights theory are based on the belief that you are not just a random collection of atoms, but a person with dignity and worth.[41] From where did this idea originate? It came from the Bible's teaching that human beings are made "in the image of God".[42] Reject God by all means, says Nietzsche, but then you must start again with new foundations, explaining why one particular creature thrown up by the blind forces of time and chance churning the primordial soup[43] for billions of years possesses inalienable rights whereas amoebae, cockroaches, and eggplants do not. I appreciate the honesty of those atheist thinkers who recognize this problem and are willing to admit that if you throw out God, with him go many other things. Novelist and atheist Llewelyn Powys wrote:

---

40   Friedrich Nietzsche, *Twilight of the Idols and The Anti-Christ*, London: Penguin, 2003 [1889], pp. 80–81.

41   Michael J. Perry, "The Morality of Human Rights: A Nonreligious Ground?", *Emory Law Journal* 54, 2005, pp. 97–150.

42   Genesis 1:26–27.

43   This is still on the menu in many motorway service stations up and down the length and breadth of the UK.

> [The atheist] must be bold to weave a bower of "endless night" upon the very edge of the abyss of abysses. This precarious cat's-cradle he must make his intellectual habitation. It is not only belief in God that must be abandoned, not only all hope of life after death, but all trust in an ordained moral order ... We must be prepared to take our bearings without a compass and with the slippery deck of our life-vessel sliding away under our feet. Dogmatic nihilists, profoundly sceptical of all good, we are put to our resources like shipwrecked seamen. We have no sense of direction, and recognise without dispute that all beyond the margin of our own scant moment is lost.[44]

If Powys is right (and many other atheists would concur with him[45]), then atheism has some far-reaching entailments. And if it does require us to dynamite the foundations with Nietzsche or toss away the compass with Powys, then that leads inexorably to the conclusion that atheism is indisputably a belief. For how could a non-belief, a non-thing, mere nothingness itself, have such drastic consequences?

⌘

So atheism looks ever more like a belief system. But there's still more evidence to consider. A further hallmark of a belief is that it attracts other beliefs to it, rather as a planet draws moons into its orbit. If I believe that learning the cello takes time and

---

44   Llewelyn Powys, *Glory of Life*, London: The Bodley Head, 1938, p. 27. See also the discussion of Powys in John Gray, *The Silence of Animals: On Progress and Other Modern Myths*, New York: Farrar, Straus and Giroux, 2013, pp. 176–207.

45   E.g. John Gray's hauntingly bleak book *Straw Dogs: Thoughts on Humans and Other Animals*, New York: Farrar, Straus and Giroux, 2003, or Bertrand Russell's classic essay, "A Free Man's Worship" (1903, the text is available on numerous websites, if one searches for the title).

diligence, then other beliefs will accumulate: I will probably believe that I should rearrange my schedule to make time to practise; that it is worth saving money for cello lessons, and so forth.[46] Similarly with my Scandinavian sceptic friend: his denial of Sweden's existence attracted other beliefs, such as a Great Global Political Conspiracy (and possibly that ABBA were really just Pink Floyd in drag). More seriously, as a Christian, my belief in God has related beliefs. I believe certain things about who Jesus was, about the purpose of life, about the limited ability of unaided human progress, about justice, values, and duties, and so forth. Beliefs attract related beliefs.

So, once again, we can ask: what about atheism? Does the statement "I do not believe in God" stand alone: stark, naked, and proud, utterly self-reliant? Or does it attract other beliefs to it; does it possess a kind of gravitational pull? Once again, it is tremendously easy to show that atheistic beliefs rarely exist in isolation. For example, most atheists believe in *naturalism*, the world view which says that only material things exist.[47] Many atheists also believe in some form of *scientism*, the belief that science can answer any and all questions both about the natural world and about the human condition. The list goes on and on. Why do so many atheists have these beliefs in common? Is it just random happenstance, like the way that folk music aficionados end up sporting beards and homemade knitwear? Not really – this cluster of beliefs is driven *by* atheism. If you believe that God does not exist, you are highly likely to believe that physics,

---

46 I studied the cello for three years at high school, but for all the wrong reasons. First, it got me out of playing rugby in winter, and second because the cello teacher was an attractive young brunette. When they replaced her with a large, bearded Russian chap, I joined the chess team instead. It was full of geeks, but at least it was inside in the warm.

47 Not to be confused with naturism. If you're planning on going into philosophy, it's vitally important to be able to spell. And to always carry a bath towel for emergencies.

chemistry, and biology can explain *everything*. You will also be tempted to pounce opportunistically on materialism as a way of keeping the divine foot out of the door.

One of the methods that astronomers sometimes use to detect distant planets, far beyond the reach of even our most powerful telescopes, is a technique called Doppler Spectroscopy, a posh name for what's more colloquially known as the "wobble method". As a planet orbits its star, gravity causes its host star to wobble slightly: detecting this allows scientists to deduce that a nearby planet is present. This is a helpful analogy for understanding atheism, for, despite Christopher Hitchens's protestation that "Our belief is not a belief", so many other beliefs are affected by atheism, drawn into its orbit as it were, that we can safely say that those who protest that atheism is not a belief do protest too much.

⌘

There is one last powerful piece of evidence that atheism really is a belief system, if not even *more* than a belief system, and that's its increasing tendency to function as an identity marker. For example, Christians gain their identity from their belief that God has revealed himself, uniquely and supremely, in and through Jesus Christ. Manchester United fans are united in their belief in their team's (usual) prowess. Supporters of the Liberal Democrat Party are united in their belief that it would be a jolly good idea to send their leader on a speaking tour of Australia. Or Azerbaijan. Or India. Or anywhere, really. This uniting under a belief is shown by the language that people use: "I am a Christian." "I am a Manchester United fan." "I am a Liberal Democrat voter."[48]

---

48   Apparently there is still one living in Chard.

We don't see anything similar happening with genuine *non*-beliefs. I have never introduced myself to anybody at a party by saying "Hello, I am an atoothfairyian". There are no university groups for disbelievers in Father Christmas, nor annual conventions for those who think that Atlantis was a myth propagated by Plato. On the other hand, many atheists do use their non-belief in God very much as an identity marker. They introduce themselves as atheists, they proudly write "freethinker" or "sceptic" in their social media profiles – with the more zealously enthusiastic changing their profile pictures to little icons of the Flying Spaghetti Monster. Furthermore, many atheists show a tendency to gather together in communities centred on their atheism. Some hang out online at places like the Richard Dawkins website in order to beat up on non-believers and remind one another how cool it is to be an atheist. They attend conferences, groups, and seminars; they buy the latest books written by atheist gurus;[49] they have creeds and accuse those who disagree with them of heresy.[50] They are even starting churches. Really, I am not making this up. In North London a few years ago, a group of atheists launched "The Sunday Assembly", where each week hundreds of people gather in a deconsecrated Anglican church to sing secular songs (such as Stevie Wonder's "Superstition") and hear messages on

---

49   One atheist friend once proudly announced to me that he had read Christopher Hitchens's book *God Is Not Great* over fifty times. That almost smacks of OCD, or "CDO", as one of my friends prefers to call it: "Because, that way, the letters are in the right darned order."

50   Atheist philosopher Thomas Nagel was deluged with thousands of angry messages, many calling him a "heretic", after his book *Mind and Cosmos* questioned several aspects of evolution and suggested that materialism could not explain several key features of reality. See Joseph Brean, "What has gotten into Thomas Nagel?: Leading atheist branded a 'heretic' for daring to question Darwinism", *National Post*, 23 March 2013 (online at http://life.nationalpost.com/2013/03/23/what-has-gotten-into-thomas-nagel-leading-atheist-branded-a-heretic-for-daring-to-question-darwinism/).

everything from science to the importance of volunteering. They then sit around and enjoy coffee and biscuits.[51]

All this raises incredible questions.[52] One concerns how long such atheist churches can function, especially as personalities and factions arise.[53] This can be difficult enough in religious communities, but at least in those cases there exists a strong "glue" that binds people together despite their differences. In the case of churches, trust in Jesus Christ is the common element that *should* unite Christians despite gender, age, politics, and fashion sense. We're even supposed to love *Star Trek* fans. But, all that aside, reflect on this question for a moment: if atheism is a non-belief, a non-claim, a non-thing, how can it perform on any level as an identity marker and as a kernel of community, however tenuous? Isn't there a much, much simpler suggestion: namely that atheism *is* a belief system and, just like other beliefs, ranging from the political to the religious, can indeed form part of a person's – or even a community's – identity.

Whichever way you consider it, atheism looks like a belief, functions like a belief, and behaves like a belief. In short: it *is* a belief. But can we go further than this? Would it be possible even to describe some forms of atheism as a *religion*? Some scholars of religion think that you can, for instance Stephen Prothero of Boston University:

51   Andrew Watts, "The church of self-worship: Sunday morning with the atheists", *The Spectator*, 22 February 2014 (http://www.spectator.co.uk/features/9141372/so-tell-me-about-your-faith-journey-sunday-morning-at-the-atheist-church/).
52   Such as whether, like churches, you can divide atheist congregations into "high" and "low" variants by the biscuits. I have long had a theory that as the doctrinal content goes down, so does the quality of the after-service snacks.
53   See e.g. "Atheist Church Split: Sunday Assembly and Godless Revival's 'Denominational Chasm'", *The Huffington Post*, 23 January 2014 (http://www.huffingtonpost.com/2014/01/06/atheist-church-split_n_4550456.html).

> Atheism is a religion of sorts, or can be. Many atheists
> are quite religious, holding their views about God with
> the conviction of zealots and evangelizing with verve ...
> It stands at the center of their lives, defining who they
> are, how they think, and with whom they associate. The
> question of God is never far from their minds.[54]

I have found that even hinting at the idea that atheism might be
a religion is a sure way to cause some atheists to go nuclear. But
here's the important thing to consider: simple disbelief in God
does not make one non-religious. There are plenty of religious
people who don't believe in God – such as many adherents of
Buddhism, Confucianism, some forms of Judaism, and most
of the Canadian United Church. To be "religious" doesn't
simply mean "to believe in God". So what does it mean? A
very helpful suggestion was once offered by sociologist Émile
Durkheim, who defined religion as "a unified system of beliefs
and practices relative to sacred things".[55] By "sacred things",
Durkheim meant anything a person holds dear, including
their ideas and values. It's really not hard to see how atheism,
especially with its temptation to fetishize science and reason,
fits this definition nicely.

There's a second way to think about the word "religion" and
that's to consider a "religion" as a system of belief that attempts
to answer ultimate questions. Is there a God? Why are we here?
How do we determine good and evil? What happens when we
die? Even the most hard-nosed, nihilistic atheist has answers
to those questions ("No"; "Time plus chance plus natural

---

54 Stephen Prothero, *God is Not One: The Eight Rival Religions That Run the World*,
New York: HarperOne, 2010, p. 326.
55 See Émile Durkheim, *The Elementary Forms of Religious Life*, Translated by Carol
Cosman with Introduction and Notes by Mark S. Cladis, Oxford: Oxford University
Press, 2008, esp. pp. xxi, 46.

selection"; "Personal preference"; "We rot", etc.) and so it fits the definition quite well. You see, here's the thing: everybody has faith; everybody is religious. Being religious is simply part of what being a human being *is*. As the French philosopher Julia Kristeva put it in a memorable book title, we all have this incredible need to believe.[56] I think that some atheists find this idea frightening, because it means there is hard thinking to be done. You can't simply say "Prove your religion to me", then cross your arms and scowl like a traffic warden with a bad case of haemorrhoids. *Everybody* has beliefs that are central for them, beliefs that cause actions, beliefs that define them, beliefs that have implications. And for those kinds of beliefs we can be asked to give reasons. If you are an atheist who wishes to duck that responsibility, then I can do no more than to commend you to one of your own, Christopher Hitchens, who said: "That which can be asserted without evidence can be dismissed without evidence."[57] Quite right too.

For Further Reading

Alain de Botton, *Religion for Atheists: A Non-Believer's Guide to the Uses of Religion* (Toronto: Signal, 2012)

Terry Eagleton, *Reason, Faith and Revolution: Reflections on the God Debate* (London: Yale University Press, 2009)

Randall Rauser, *The Swedish Atheist, the Scuba Diver and Other Apologetic Rabbit Trails* (Downers Grove, IL: IVP, 2012)

Chris Stedman, *Faitheist: How an Atheist Found Common Ground with the Religious* (Boston, MA: Beacon Press, 2012)

---

56   Julia Kristeva, *The Incredible Need to Believe*, New York: Columbia University Press, 2011. See also Christian Smith, *Moral, Believing Animals: Human Personhood and Culture*, Oxford: Oxford University Press, 2003.
57   Hitchens, *God Is Not Great*, p. 50.

3

The Aardvark in the Artichokes

(or: Why Not All Gods are the Same)

"They're *gooooonnnnnnneeeeeeee!*" A low, mournful wail rose above the wooden fence. I dropped my bag of shopping, raced across the road, stood on tiptoe and peered into the garden from where the cry had come. A large man, clad in overalls and carrying a spade, was kneeling in the middle of a flowerbed, sobbing and howling.

"Is everything OK?" I asked, with typical British understatement.

The man wiped his eyes with grubby hands, covering his face with soil in the process. This, with the tear-stained effect, made him look like a somewhat startled badger.

"They're *gooooonnnnnnneeeeeeee!*" he repeated, and let out another series of convulsive sobs.

"What are gone?" I asked gently.

Half an hour and two boxes of tissues later, I had the full story. Apparently, Brian was quite the gardener and had been growing an extensive selection of plants and vegetables for display at the forthcoming village fête. Potentially prize-winning petunias, enormous eggplants, magnificent marigolds, colossal cabbages, and nasturtiums to which no superlative could do justice.[58] However, during the hours of darkness, some creature of the night had snuck into his garden and munched the lot. Now, just a sad collection of stems and half-chewed pieces of petal were all he had to show for his horticultural efforts.

"Parish Council banned pesticides, slug pellets, and land mines," Brian sniffed. "It's all *their* fault."

"You think slugs did this?" I asked. "Look, I'm no gardener (although I did once meet Alan Titchmarsh[59] when he was opening a supermarket), but I think that this looks more like the work of a bigger creature."

Brian scratched his balding head and looked thoughtful. "You mean some kind of mammal? Nah, I can't see it myself. Aardvarks don't live in Somerset and they're non-migratory ..."

"Aardvarks in the artichokes?" I said. "No, I was thinking more of – "

" – panthers? Well, there have long been rumours of mysterious black cats roaming the moors, but polishing off my petunias?"

"Again, I wasn't thinking of panthers. Or indeed anything quite *that* big. I was thinking more of ..." With my toe, I nudged one of the round, black droppings littered suspiciously across the lawn. Brian picked one up, rolled it between his fingers, and sniffed it carefully.

"Not a chocolate drop, I take it?" I said.

"Sheep?" he said. "You think a sheep hopped over my fence and scoffed my strawberries?"

---

58   At least not alliteratively.
59   Other nations may have sporting heroes and movie stars; England has celebrity gardeners. I think that tells you much of what you need to know about the English.

"No," I said wearily, "not a sheep, but maybe a r – "

" – eindeer? A reindeer raided my radishes? I find that hard to believe. There'd be hoofprints."

And so it went on for the next twenty minutes. Unable to get a word in edgeways, I gave up and let Brian rattle off a multitudinous menagerie of mammals – antelopes to leopards to zebras – and, in each case, offer an explanation for why *they* couldn't have guzzled his garden. Finally, he paused for breath.

"Rabbits!" I yelled.

"Where? I'll get my gun!" said Brian, leaping to his feet.

"No, I mean *rabbits* ate your vegetables."

Brian looked thoughtful for a moment. "No, I don't buy it."

"But it explains *everything*, wouldn't you say?" I pleaded. "Trust me, it was rabbits!"

"Who's the expert gardener here?" Brian retorted huffily. "Look, you've agreed that it wasn't any of these mammals I listed; you've dismissed every single one of them. Well, I just go one mammal further than you and deny the rabbit, too. If you were consistent, you'd agree. Now then – fancy a chocolate drop?"

⌘

Bafflingly bizarre as Brian's argument sounds, versions of it exist in the wild. For example, it bears an uncanny resemblance to one particular claim that has been advanced by some contemporary atheists. Known as the "One God Less" argument, an illustrative specimen occurs in this paragraph from Richard Dawkins's *The God Delusion*:

> I have found it an amusing strategy, when asked whether I am atheist, to point out that the questioner is also an atheist when considering Zeus, Apollo, Amon Ra,

Mithras, Baal, Thor, Wotan, the Golden Calf and the Flying Spaghetti Monster. I just go one god further.[60]

To describe this as a bad argument is to flirt somewhat casually with understatement. Dawkins is, for example, a *bachelor* with regard to every other woman except his wife, but I am not sure that it would be entirely fair on that basis to deny existence to Mrs Dawkins. Similarly, Dawkins is also a *non-resident* with regard to every city in the world other than Oxford, but that doesn't mean he can call himself homeless and start claiming government benefits. In short, the argument leaks like a rusty colander, and were it not for the fact that it has multiplied around the Internet, reproducing like rabbits in spring, it might be better just to let it die a death. However, this particular bad argument is actually quite useful because it opens up the opportunity to talk about something quite important: namely the often-overlooked fact that all religions are *not* the same, all gods are *not* equal, and the differences make a difference.

But, first, let's warm up by shooting some fish in a barrel. What, precisely, is wrong in the story of Brian's gardening tragedy and also with Richard Dawkins's "One God Less" argument? I suspect most people instantly sense that, despite the clever rhetoric, there is something suspicious going on, but what *precisely*? Well, here's the problem: if Brian and Richard are right, then whenever we need to select one candidate from a range of possible answers, we can't, because somebody can always heckle us with cries of "You rejected everything else; why settle on this one answer?" Yet filtering out the *right* answer from a set of *wrong* answers is the way that we proceed to uncover truth in a wide variety of fields – in fact in *most* of life, *most* of the time.

---

60 Dawkins, *The God Delusion*, p. 77.

Consider crime for a moment. In fact, to bring it even more down to earth, consider one of my favourite childhood board games, *Cluedo*.[61] The excitement kicks off with the discovery of a corpse, the hapless Mr Black, lying dead at the foot of the cellar steps. Players then proceed to while away a happy hour playing at being detectives, deducing which of the six possible suspects killed the victim, with which weapon, in which room of Mr Black's extensive country pile.[62] By the careful elimination of false hypotheses, the sifting of evidence, and the piecing-together of clues, finally the dastardly murderer stands exposed. But here's the thing: let's imagine that an armchair detective has skilfully sleuthed that Colonel Mustard committed the vile deed. At which point the moustachioed military man pipes up and says: "Now hang on, old boy! Reverend Green, Miss Scarlett, Professor Plum, Mrs White, and Mrs Peacock are *all* innocent. So I suggest you just go 'one character more' and let me go free." How would we reply? I think we would respond that the fact that those other five characters didn't whack Mr Black over the head with the lead piping has nothing whatsoever to say about Colonel Mustard's innocence. Indeed, it is the very nature of the game of *Cluedo* that we are looking for *one* murderer, *one* weapon, *one* room among a larger set of possibilities.

Just as in the board game, this is how the investigation of crime proceeds in the real world. The police are faced with a range of possible suspects and, one by one, each is eliminated until the guilty party is identified. So, again, imagine what would happen were that individual to stand before a judge and protest: "Your Honour, I've been discriminated against! The

---

61   The game is known as *Clue* in many parts of the world.
62   I'm convinced that it's the export of *Cluedo* that has led many Americans to the apparently ingrained belief that every English home possesses a billiard room, a library, and a plethora of secret passages. And we also all know the Queen personally, of course.

police were sceptical about the guilt of ten other people, yet they arrested me! Your Honour, I encourage you to release one suspect more." My hunch is that this defence might possibly qualify the accused for one of those more specialized penal institutions where the prison overalls have those nice, handy sleeves that strap at the back and the cells come with the thoughtful addition of rubber wallpaper. The argument is, to use a technical term from academic philosophy, bonkers.

Not merely does the "One God Less" argument completely erode the process of law, it also has astonishing side effects when it comes to Dawkins's own beloved area of science. Many people are confused about how science works.[63] We think of bespectacled scientists, dressed in pristine white coats, engaged in exciting experiments in laboratories full of flickering machinery and bubbling test tubes. Occasionally there is a loud shout of excitement,[64] and some new discovery is made – weeks of careful experiment and observation have paid off. Now, that is *sometimes* how science proceeds, especially in the movies. There are, however, many fields of science where nothing like that ever happens: disciplines such as evolutionary biology and cosmology, for example. In those areas, progress is made as theories and models are suggested and those that best explain the data are adopted by scientists. Often there are competing theories jostling for position, but over time the truth emerges, leaving failed hypotheses to fall by the wayside.[65] So what, I wonder, would Dawkins say to somebody who were to accost him in Oxford High Street and announce: "I say, Professor

63 My mother, for example. As a child, I was entirely unable to convince her that experiments in the kitchen involving things like vinegar, bicarbonate of soda, battery acid, and her best saucepan were science and were thus exempt from the normal rules.
64 Or terror, if it's chemistry.
65 See the classic Thomas S. Kuhn, *The Structure of Scientific Revolutions*, London: University of Chicago Press, 1970.

Dawkins, you're wrong, completely wrong, about evolution!"

"Another damnable creationist," the former Simonyi Professor for the Public Understanding of Science would mutter, scarcely breaking his stride.

"I'm *not* a creationist," the passer-by retorts. "I'm a biologist, just like you. Also just like you, I've rejected Pangenesis, Lamarckian Inheritance, and Punctuated Equilibrium. But, unlike you, I'm a more *consistent* sceptic. Indeed, I just go 'One Theorem Further' and also deny Natural Selection."

You see, the underlying problem with the "One God Less" argument is that it *goes too far*. If the argument were valid, it would have a devastating consequence, namely that it would behave like a universal acid and erode all exclusive truth claims, be they in theology, law, or science.[66] In any situation where we want to claim that X is true, but not Y or Z, the sceptic could wave their hands and cry "Foul". So are we stuck? No, because Dawkins has made a fairly basic mistake, namely failing to notice that when multiple explanations are offered for something – be that a murder, a scientific theory, or a religious claim – we don't immediately assume that all are *equally* likely. Should my wife enter the kitchen and discover the cookie jar to be empty of all but crumbs, there are a number of possibilities. For instance, it is not entirely impossible that a many-limbed alien from Betelgeuse IV teleported in and munched them, perhaps owing to a biscuit shortage in his own galaxy. Or one could conceive of a scenario in which our elderly neighbour, slightly tipsy from overdoing the gin and tonic at her bridge club, snuck in while I was mowing the lawn and purloined them. Then again, it's also possible that I showed my usual lack of restraint when in the presence of processed sugary foods,

66   See Edward Feser, *The Last Superstition: A Refutation of the New Atheism*, South Bend, IN: St. Augustine's Press, 2012, pp. 199–221.

and snaffled the lot. If we had time, we could dream up other scenarios, I'm sure. However, I know which one my wife would pick. Only a complete fool (or somebody guiltily brushing the cookie crumbs from his shirt) would try to claim that *every* possible explanation is equally likely.

⌘

So when we are faced with a range of possible explanations – aliens *or* hungry husbands, Miss Scarlett *or* Colonel Mustard, aardvarks *or* rabbits, the Flying Spaghetti Monster *or* God – what should we do? If it's wrong to reject all of them equally, it's likewise wrong simply to flip a coin or spin a wheel.[67] Instead, what we should do is what rational, normal, intelligent people do all the time. Fire up Wikipedia. Sorry, I meant look at the evidence. It often comes as a shock to many atheists to know that there is surprisingly good evidence for God, not least because many religious folks, in between the book burnings, inquisitions, and causing plague, pestilence, and war that occupy the daylight hours for most of us,[68] have actually spent time thinking. Now this is not the place to explore all the evidence for the existence of God, but, for those who wish to meander down that particular avenue, the eminent and bespectacled American philosopher Alvin Plantinga has sketched out two dozen arguments for God's existence that you can peruse at your leisure.[69]

67   Back in my days as a university lecturer, I used to have an Instant Essay Assessment Wheel (a little spinning pointer and a circle divided into "Pass", "Third", "Second", and "First") pinned to my office wall. The principal of the college asked me to take it down, apparently because it was disturbing students, which I always thought was the point of higher education. Most lecturers now just use an app. Much more discreet.

68   That was satire. Or, as a Canadian friend's ten-year-old son defined it: "Telling lies in a funny way with an English accent."

69   Alvin Plantinga, "Two Dozen (or so) Theistic Arguments", available online at: http://bit.ly/plantinga24. At a more popular level, I can also recommend C. S. Lewis,

But "Aha!" exclaims Richard Dawkins (who has just had a magnificent dinner accompanied by a simply superb bottle of Château Lafite-Rothschild Pauillac '96, and so is feeling in beneficently emollient mood) "Even were I to grant you that some of those arguments might possibly work, the question is which god. The world is liberally littered with gods; there is a multifarious diversity of deities. You believe that Yahweh is god, Andy, but there's Allah, Baal, Chemosh, Dagon, Enki, even our old friend the Flying Spaghetti Monster. I'll stop at the Fs. Why on earth should I believe that Yahweh is real – when even you accept that all the others, this gargantuan galaxy of gods, are all false?"

Now that's a great question. But it's based on a massive and fundamental category error, one that I believe a hobbit of all things can help us to clear up.[70] Let's imagine that those mischievous young scamps, Peregrin Took and Meriadoc Brandybuck, are sitting one day in the sunshine outside The Green Dragon, puffing away on pipe-weed and enjoying a quiet beer. Suddenly, Peregrin comes over all philosophical.

"Merry," he asks thoughtfully, "have you ever wondered who created Middle Earth?"

His hairy-footed drinking companion thoughtfully blows a smoke ring. "That's a good question, Pippin my friend. A tough question, to be sure. Let me think now – maybe it was the elves?"

"I wondered about that at first," Pippin replied. "But then Galadriel and her people have their schedules pretty busy doing their hair and bleaching their robes – that look takes

---

Mere Christianity, Glasgow: Collins, 1990, and Timothy Keller, The Reason for God, London: Hodder & Stoughton, 2008.

70   My apologies in advance to Middle Earth fans should Peter Jackson turn the following illustration into a nine-hour movie (although I believe that two old shopping lists of Tolkien's that have recently been discovered behind a bookcase at Pembroke College, Oxford are due to be turned into a four-part epic first).

work. So making the whole of Middle Earth on the side? Can't see it myself …"

"Perhaps Gandalf, then?" mused Merry, supping his beer.

"Again, our wizardly friend carries many secrets, but I don't see him creating universes in his spare time."

Merry thought hard again for a few moments. "Well … what about this for an idea? Isn't the whole point of *The Lord of the Rings* – "

"The which-of-the-what?"

"*The Lord of the Rings*. It's the book we're in. I'm using a clever postmodern literary device and breaking the fourth wall – "

"I see," said Pippin, who didn't and was beginning to feel that this whole conversation was going to be an epic.

"Isn't the whole point of *The Lord of the Rings* that the weakest, the smallest, the most unlikely character turns out to be central to everything?"

Pippin looked startled. "Frodo? You're suggesting Frodo created Middle Earth? Heavens above, his ego is big enough what with defeating evil, saving the world, and starting that successful chain of spider burger restaurants, but if he found out he created the world? I shudder to think."

"You're probably right," said Merry. "Time for another beer?"

Aside from causing Professor Tolkien to spin in his grave, what's the point of that illustration? Well, it's that if they were looking for the creator of Middle Earth, Merry and Pippin were barking up entirely the wrong tree by considering characters *inside* the story. They could explore every street in Hobbiton, climb every peak of the Misty Mountains, enlist the help of every elf and dwarf from here to Rohan, but they wouldn't find Tolkien inside The Lord of the Rings. What's the difference between Thorin, Théoden, Treebeard, and Tolkien? The first three are characters, created by the writer. The last is the author himself. And if you caught me speaking of Aragorn and Tolkien in the same breath, you'd probably conclude that I'd had one too many pints of Barliman's Best.

Something similar is going on with the "One God Less" argument. When certain atheists include "God" in one of those notoriously quixotic lists they love rattling off – including him along with Zeus, Thor, the Flying Spaghetti Monster, and even Bertrand Russell's famous invisible floating teapot – they're making a tremendous category mistake, because every single one of those other entities is an object inside the universe. God, on the other hand, according to Christianity is the creator and sustainer of the universe, the author of the story. Listen to how David Bentley Hart puts this:

> [God, capital "G"] is not a "being", at least not in the way that a tree, a shoemaker or a god is a being; he is not one more object in the inventory of things that are, or any sort of discrete object at all. Rather, all things that exist receive their being continuously from him, who is the infinite wellspring of all that is, *in whom* (to use the language of the Christian scriptures) all things live and move and have their being.[71]

One of the things that moving to Canada taught me was the importance of being careful with language. People and cultures can use words in *very* different ways. Shortly after we arrived in Toronto, my wife and I had our first appointment with our immigration lawyer. We entered his office to discover an elderly, 350-pound gentleman, sitting behind the largest oak desk I

---

71   David Bentley Hart, *The Experience of God: Being, Consciousness, Bliss*, New Haven: Yale University Press, 2013, p. 30.

have ever seen. His opening words to us were: "Please excuse me for not standing up to shake your hand, but I'm not wearing pants today." Now you may be aware that "pants" is one of those words that loses something in transatlantic translation – and so for the whole meeting, we tried to put the image of this huge man, naked from the waist down, out of our minds. Finally, at the end of our time together, he rose from his seat on trembling legs and all was revealed, or rather wasn't.

"Again, forgive my wearing shorts," he said, "I had varicose vein surgery yesterday". We resisted the urge to send him the bill for the therapy.

Words can mean very different things to different people. The fact that Richard Dawkins can use the word "god" to denote the whole pluralistic pantheon of ancient Greece and Rome, for instance, tells me that he does not mean the same thing by it as Christians do. It is very clear, for instance, that in Greco-Roman mythology Zeus and Apollo, Mercury and Mithras were *creatures* within the world. By all means, they had special powers, but they were mere beings – they were part of the created order, not responsible for bringing reality itself into existence. In one sense, those "gods" were just like very big versions of us. And here I realize that one reason for Dawkins's confusion may be the somewhat lackadaisical way that Christians sometimes talk about God – as if he is our friend, our buddy, our mate, basically just like a big person who resides "up there" somewhere. The stereotypical view of God as the kindly old gentleman with the beard who lives in the clouds may be just that – a stereotype – but it is one that, to be fair to my atheist friends, Christians have sometimes helped to propagate through linguistic laziness and theological ineptitude.

But God is not a thing, not an object, not a person like you and me, only bigger. God is, according to 2,000 years of more thoughtful Christian tradition, the source of all being, the one who creates and sustains all things, the reason that *anything* exists at all.[72] He is also the ultimate source of mind, the ground of all truth, the foundation of goodness and beauty. The Flying Spaghetti Monster, if such a noodly-appendaged creature existed, is precisely that: a *creature*. Presumably one could explore his ways using science, because science is remarkably good at investigating material things. On the other hand, the God of Christianity is a very different matter entirely – he is the reason we exist, can experience, can think, can ask questions, and can do science in the first place. Indeed, as somebody once remarked, even to argue against God is to tacitly admit that he exists. What do I mean? Well, to argue against God, to write books like *The God Delusion*, is to admit that truth is important (otherwise, why does it matter what somebody believes?). It's to claim that pursuing knowledge is a virtue (otherwise, why choose the hard truth over a comfortable lie?). It's to claim that justice matters (Dawkins's book is a profoundly moral tract, even offering us an atheist ten commandments). But truth, the pursuit of knowledge, the existence of ultimate values such as justice – those are grounded, ultimately, in God. And so to pick these things up and wield them as weapons against God is *to play by his rules*. A far more consistent atheist position

---

72 I occasionally encounter enthusiastic young atheists who inform me that physicists can explain, using science alone, why there is a universe at all, why there is something rather than nothing. A commonly quoted work in this regard is Lawrence M. Krauss's *A Universe From Nothing*, New York: Free Press, 2012. In a nutshell, his argument is: (a) Nothing isn't really nothing, but is really a kind of something; (b) Science can tell us a lot about something; (c) Therefore we don't need God. You may accuse me of simplistic parody here, but quite seriously that's the argument and many reviewers (including fellow atheists) have called him out on it, pointing out that the book is woefully mistitled, since it doesn't answer the question at all. Indeed, as I occasionally remark to my atheist interlocutors, if nothing really is a kind of something, try that as an excuse next time you fail to produce a gift come Valentine's Day or your Significant Other's birthday. ("But, darling, nothing really is a kind of something; Dr Krauss said so …")

would instead be to toss those things away as philosophical flotsam and jetsam and to embrace absurdity. It might not be a comfortable place to live, but at least it would have the merit of not being inherently self-contradictory.

⌘

The "One God Less" argument is now twitching spasmodically but it's not quite dead, for a slightly more nuanced form of it occasionally pops up. Here's an example, from a popular atheist blog that once had this as its masthead: "When you understand why you dismiss all the other possible gods, you will understand why I dismiss yours." This is slightly cleverer than the Dawkins flavour of the argument: it says – with a sneer or an avuncular air, depending on the tone in which you read it – "Look, if you just thought like *me*, you'd be an atheist. Come on, be *reasonable* ... " This may not be as outright absurd as its rabbit-denying cousin, but does it work any better? Well, not really. The first problem is that even this form of the argument still functions as a universal acid, eroding atheism as much as religion. How so? Well, we saw in chapter two that atheism is itself a belief system, so let's reword the aphorism this way: "When you understand why I dismiss all other belief systems, you will understand why I dismiss atheism." In other words, if one goes down this route the only consistent position is abject nihilism, the view that everything is utterly, entirely, cosmically meaningless.[73]

But there's another problem with this form of the "One God Less" argument. It assumes, entirely uncritically, that the world's myriad of religions are all essentially the same.

---

73 Try watching daytime television for couple of mornings and you'll begin to get a sense of how this feels.

The atheist making this claim has not investigated all of them – probably not *any* of them – and is instead assuming that they must all be more or less similar to the characterless Catholicism or pedestrian Protestantism they half-remember from their youth, their schooldays, or their grandparents, or from what they've gleaned from the entirely fair and balanced presentation of Christianity served up, lukewarm, by the media. Well, we know all about *that*, so we can dismiss everything else – after all, every religion is essentially the same, isn't it? I find it fascinating that many atheists suddenly look like Unitarian Universalists[74] at this point, claiming that all religions teach the same thing, so therefore we can't possibly discriminate between them.

Well, we can and I did. For a long series of reasons that I won't bore you with (which involved a wet weekend in Peckham, followed by 300 hecklers, a stepladder, and several plates of Kentucky Fried Chicken), I ended up studying Islam for twenty years and getting a PhD in Qur'anic Studies.[75] One of the discoveries that fascinated me the most in my doctoral research was that Allah, the God of the Qur'an, is startlingly different from Yahweh, the God of the Bible. Indeed, on almost every major point of Christian doctrine, I think it is safe to say that Islam teaches the opposite. This is not to pick on my Muslim friends, simply to recognize that their religion is very *different*. If you're going to become an expert in the philosophy of Immanuel Kant, you won't get far by reading David Hume

---

74   I once talked to a Unitarian Universalist at the University of Toronto who stressed that the way to achieve harmony between different religions and belief systems was to avoid talking about things like fact, truth, and certainty. "If I ever find myself more than 60 per cent certain about anything," he confessed, "I get very nervous." I was too polite to ask: "Are you more than 60 per cent certain of that statement?"

75   If you're super-keen, you can even read the academic book it turned into: Andrew G. Bannister, *An Oral-Formulaic Study of the Qur'an*, New York: Lexington Books, 2014.

and protesting that "All dead philosophers said the same thing". The differences really do make a difference.

Among the major differences between Islam and Christianity is that of the character and nature of God as understood by the Bible and the Qur'an. For the Bible, Yahweh is a *relational* God, a God who appears to his people throughout the Old Testament, who took on flesh in the incarnation of Jesus Christ in the New Testament, and who will be present, the Bible claims, in heaven with us once again: "For now we see through a glass, darkly," wrote the apostle Paul; "but then face to face".[76] This is very different from Allah in the Qur'an, a God who is distant and remote, transcendent and lofty, who does not deign to step down into his creation, and is not present in Paradise. As Muslim theologian Isma'il al Faruqi writes:

> Allah does not reveal Himself to anyone in any way. Allah reveals only his will ... Allah does not reveal himself to anyone ... that is the great difference between Christianity and Islam.[77]

Central, too, to the Christian understanding of God is that Yahweh is loving; indeed, the Bible goes as far as to boldly make the claim that God *is* love,[78] the one whose character and nature define what love actually is. You will commonly hear people opine that *all* religions teach that God is love, but this is simply not true – for instance, nowhere does the Qur'an claim that "Allah is love".[79]

---

76   1 Corinthians 13:12 (KJV).
77   Isma'il al Faruqi, *Christian Mission and Islamic Da'wah: Proceedings of the Chambésy Dialogue Consultation*, Leicester: The Islamic Foundation, 1982, pp. 47–48.
78   1 John 4:16.
79   And many Muslim theologians argue that Muslims should not use the word "love" when talking about Allah; see e.g. Murad Wilfried Hofmann, "Differences between the Muslim and the Christian Concept of Divine Love" in 14th General Conference

Finally, at the heart of Christianity stands the belief that, in Jesus, God has experienced suffering, paying the price of the cross in order to reconcile humanity to himself. Now atheists may choose to dismiss, laugh at, or even scoff at that claim, but it is a claim unique to Christianity.[80] It is certainly not an idea found in Islam, where the Qur'an goes as far as to deny that the historical event of Jesus' crucifixion ever happened.

It has long fascinated me that when Christianity talks about the cross and the suffering of God, it is doing something quite startling, namely reversing the traffic pattern of every other religion, world view, and belief system. All other religions of which I am aware tend to work in one of three basic ways: they claim that if you *know* the right things, *do* the right things, or *experience* the right things, then you will achieve paradise, nirvana, wisdom, a higher state of consciousness, good teeth – whatever it is you are looking for. Islam adopts this model ("Keep the commandments"), as does, incidentally, the New Atheism, whose message is that if you think the right way – think good, secular, scientific thoughts – you'll be one of the smart ones, one of the brights,[81] one of the elite, the elect. (Of course, there's then a rather dangerous temptation that you'll look snootily

---

of the Royal Aal al-Bayt Institute for Islamic Thought, Amman, Jordan, 2007 (online at http://www.aalalbayt.org/ar/ResearchDocuments/14.pdf). See also Gordon Nickel, "The Language of Love in Qur'ān and Gospel" in Juan Pedro Monferrer-Sala and Ángel Urbán, (eds), *Sacred Text: Explorations in Lexicography*, Frankfurt: Peter Lang, 2009, pp. 223–248 (online at https://www.academia.edu/2105679/The_Language_of_Love_in_Quran_and_Gospel).

80　If you wish to understand this idea (which, whatever you make of it, is the central claim at the heart of Christianity), a great place to start is John Stott, *The Cross of Christ*, Leicester: IVP, 2006.

81　A nauseatingly self-congratulatory term coined by some of the New Atheists to mark themselves off from the rest of the world, whom they clearly perceive as dimwits. See Daniel Dennett, "The Bright Stuff", *The New York Times*, 12 July 2003 (http://www.nytimes.com/2003/07/12/opinion/the-bright-stuff.html).

down your nose at everybody else who is not as clever or as enlightened as you are.)

The uncanny similarities between the New Atheism and certain forms of Islam are not just restricted to the question of how one is "saved". There is another overlap, too, and that concerns rigidity and inflexibility. Now of course every world view has its fundamentalist flavours but in some that flavour has marinated through the whole somewhat more: witness what is going on in the Middle East right now, for instance. When Islamic fundamentalism gets wedded to a political vision of reality then the results can be tragic, for both Muslims and religious (and non-religious) minorities.[82] But some atheists have a political vision of reality too, one that equally dances upon the precipitous edge of totalitarianism: for instance, when we hear an atheist like Sam Harris write dreamily of his hopes for a secular world government, which we may have to arrive at by a series of "benign dictatorships",[83] we should quite naturally begin to worry. Perhaps what we need is not so much one *god* less as one *fundamentalism* less, secular or otherwise.

For Further Reading

David Bentley Hart, *The Experience of God: Being, Consciousness, Bliss* (New Haven: Yale University Press, 2013)

Abdu H. Murray, *Grand Central Question: Answering the Critical Concerns of the Major Worldviews* (Downers Grove, IL: IVP, 2014)

Ellis Potter, *3 Theories of Everything* (Huemoz: Destinée Media, 2012)

---

82 Robert Reilly argues in his book *The Closing of the Muslim Mind* (Wilmington: Intercollegiate Studies Institute, 2010) that the problem is not necessarily Islam per se, but a narrowly legalistic and uncritical form of it that historically took root as the mainstream.

83 Sam Harris, *The End of Faith*, London: The Free Press, 2006, p. 151.

Stephen Prothero, *God is Not One: The Eight Rival Religions That Run the World* (New York: HarperOne, 2010)

Nabeel Qureshi, *Seeking Allah, Finding Jesus: A Devout Muslim Encounters Christianity* (Grand Rapids, MI: Zondervan, 2014)

4

The Santa Delusion

(or: Why Faith in God Does Not Mean You're Insane)

Let me paint a scene for you, so sink into a comfortable seat, relax, and close your eyes. Actually, that will prevent you from reading further, so you'd better open them again. Now, I'd like you to imagine that you are a fly on a wall of a brightly lit, modern office, somewhere in the leafy suburbs of North London. These are the offices of Richard Dawkins's literary agent, and, over a cup of coffee and a plate of Jammie Dodgers,[84] a frank discussion is being had about sales figures.[85]

"It's not good news, Richard," says the agent. "I'm afraid they're not going to reprint *The Selfish Gene* and plans to launch a range of action figures based on you and Lawrence Krauss have come to naught."

---

84 One of the geniuses of British invention, up there with the steam engine, the thermos flask, and television, a Jammie Dodger consists of two layers of biscuit, glued together with a combination of cream and jam. Everybody gets excited about composite materials in aviation; we British have had them in biscuits since the 1960s.

85 I owe some of the inspiration for this scene to David Mitchell and Robert Webb's comedy sketch: http://bit.ly/dawkinsagent.

Dawkins splutters into his coffee, spilling some of it on his necktie. He's proud of the tie, bearing as it does a picture of the DNA molecule. ("Very fetching, dear," Mrs Dawkins had said, when he'd spent forty minutes explaining that it wasn't just *any* old piece of DNA, but the precise coding sequence for haemoglobin.)

"What about my children's book?" Dawkins demands. "That *must* be selling well. There's good money in kids' books! J. K. Rowling had to change banks, on account of filling the first one up."

His agent shuffles his papers in an embarrassed way. "Well ... the problem is that *your* book, lovely as the pictures are, well ... it doesn't have wizards or flying donkeys in it. That's the basic problem, Richard."

"But it's *science!*"

"Well, it isn't *selling.*"

A silence falls on the room. Both men eye the last of the Jammie Dodgers.

"What about my autobiography?" Dawkins asks. "Didn't *Salon* magazine list me as the seventh sexiest man alive? My cover photograph on the book must surely have shifted a few copies? I even saw a woman buying a copy at Tesco."

"Again, it's not good news," says the agent, stealing a furtive glance at his watch.

"Not good – well, what about the film version? You did get my message asking you to ring a few – "

" – people who might play you? As you requested, I've left *multiple* messages for Sir Ian McKellen, but he's not returning any of my calls."

Dawkins harrumphs in a way that only years of practice as an Oxford don can train you for. "Is there *any* good news?"

"Well …" His agent rummages through a sheaf of papers on his lap. "I do have one thing that could be promising. I've a letter here from Butlins – "

"*Butlins!*"

"Yes, the holiday-camp people. They're offering you a three-week run in Skegness if you could write a version of *The Extended Phenotype* as a musical."

Dawkins snatches the last Jammie Dodger and bites into it angrily.

"The problem", his agent explains nervously, "is that all your material is a bit – well, a bit *last year*. You've demolished creationism and popularized evolution. You've done the whole anti-God thing. But now people want something new. The iconoclasm and the consensus-smashing is all very well, but you need to find a new vein of disbelief to tap into."

"Well, it's funny you should say that," Dawkins replies, dabbing the jam from his chin with a handkerchief. "I do have one idea brewing …"

"Fantastic! Let's hear it!" says his agent, leaning forward eagerly.

"It may need a little work, but what do you think … what do you think about *The Santa Delusion*?"

"The *what*?"

"*The Santa Delusion.*"

"Are you serious?"

"Very much so. Santa is a deleterious delusion, one peddled every year to innocent children by their parents, backed up by the forces of the mass media. It's time to put some reason into the season."

The agent puts his head in his hands.

"I can see you're not thrilled," says Dawkins, rubbing his

palms together and warming to his theme, "but I've *really* been thinking about this. Father Christmas is one of the most unpleasant characters in all fiction. Gluttonous and proud of it. A wine-bibbing, sherry-swigging, mince-pie-gobbling freak. An elf-exploiting, reindeer-rights-abusing bully. A consumeristic, materialistic, atavistic, patriarchal, nationalistic myth. A – "

"I get the point," interrupts the agent.

"So do you think it could be a best seller?" asks Dawkins eagerly.

The agent reaches for the phone. "Let me call Butlins back. Skegness in June can be quite lovely …"

⌘

Of course, Richard Dawkins never did write *The Santa Delusion*. Nor has he felt the need to pen *The Fairy Fallacy*, or to draft *The Thomas the Tank Engine Trick*. Why do I mention these? Because he, like many of his fellow atheists, loves to bracket belief in God with belief in a whole host of fictional and mythical entities, suggesting that they are somehow comparable. Let me give you a flavour:

> A beautiful child close to me, six and the apple of her father's eye, believes that Thomas the Tank Engine really exists. She believes in Father Christmas, and when she grows up her ambition is to be a tooth fairy. She and her schoolfriends believe the solemn word of respected adults that tooth fairies and Father Christmas really exist. This little girl is of an age to believe whatever you tell her. If you tell her about witches changing princes into frogs, she will believe you. If you tell her that bad children roast forever in hell, she will have nightmares.

> I have just discovered that without her father's consent
> this sweet, trusting, gullible six-year-old is being sent, for
> weekly instruction, to a Roman Catholic nun.[86]

As the father of a two-year-old, I can partly understand the concern about Thomas the Tank Engine, as I have already heard enough stories of the loveable locomotive (many *several* times) to long for the day when modernization comes to the Island of Sodor and everything goes electric. Still, I digress. It's particularly the comparison with Santa Claus and the Tooth Fairy that I find the most fascinating. It's a theme to which Dawkins regularly returns. Here he is again:

> Father Christmas and the Tooth Fairy are part of the charm
> of childhood. So is God. Some of us grow out of all three.[87]

At least that is, to give credit where it's due, slightly more generous. God is a charming childish fantasy, rather than a wicked lie used by malicious Catholic nuns to wrap their insidious tentacles around innocent children. Now Dawkins is not the only one to compare God to Santa Claus; for example, here is another of the New Atheists, Daniel Dennett:

> The kindly God who lovingly fashioned each and every
> one of us (all creatures great and small) and sprinkled
> the sky with shining stars for our delight – *that* God
> is, like Santa Claus, a myth of childhood, not anything a
> sane, undeluded adult could literally believe in. *That* God
> must either be turned into a symbol for something less
> concrete or abandoned altogether.[88]

86 Richard Dawkins, *A Devil's Chaplain: Selected Writings*, London: Phoenix, 2004, p. 151.
87 Quoted in *Third Way* magazine , Vol. 26, No. 5, June 2003, p. 5.
88 Daniel Dennett, *Darwin's Dangerous Idea: Evolution and the Meanings of Life*, London: Simon & Schuster, 1996, p. 18.

Powerful language, whose polemical sneer is not entirely mitigated by the defence that the author is attacking naïve, simplistic forms of religious faith. Maybe belief in the distant shadowy deity of an insipid deism might just be permissible for Dennett, but anything else is deluded. One last example of the genre, and then we will explore whether this whole "God is like Santa Claus" argument stands up. This final exhibit was penned by psychologist Nigel Barber in *The Huffington Post* and is instructive because it singles out those whom these atheists really think are responsible – the pernicious parents who pass on these beliefs:

> Similarly, in religious countries, people may well stop believing in Santa Claus when they grow up but still hang on to their religious belief system. So it takes more than skepticism to separate people from their religious faith. Why do religious people trash some implausible beliefs but keep others? Perhaps they get something out of the beliefs they keep. Once a person grows up, their parents no longer shower them with gifts during the holiday season, so they have no particular reason to sustain their credulity concerning Santa Claus, although they do pass on the belief to children.[89]

Well there you have it. If my parents had continued buying me *Star Wars* action figures and Meccano™ well into my teens, I'd still believe in Santa. However, poor, deluded fool that I am, I continue to believe in God, despite the fact that it marks me out as childish. Whatever shall we do? I guess a good place to begin is by illustrating what a disastrous argument this is on many levels.

---

89 Nigel Barber, "Why Believe in God but Not Santa Claus?", *Huffington Post*, 21 February 2014 (http://www.huffingtonpost.com/nigel-barber/why-believe-in-god-but-not-santa-claus_b_4816026.html).

The first problem is that it's a classic example of an *ad hominem* fallacy. That is when, rather than critique an argument or belief, you attack the person making it. For example, I might say that all of Nigel Barber's arguments are wrong because he is a funny-looking chap who only writes for *The Huffington Post* because he can't get published in a proper newspaper and that he did a degree in psychology rather than one of the hard sciences (e.g. biology, chemistry or macramé[90]) because he hadn't got the necessary grades. I might add that psychology is, as everybody knows, the modern-day equivalent of alchemy and phrenology and so we can dismiss anything said by a "psychologist" as quackery.

See what I did there? I used ridicule and insult to dismiss the *person*, rather than address what they were *saying*. And the primary problem with doing this is that it's terribly lazy. How easy it is to insult somebody's looks, to sneer at their academic credentials, to deride their inability to tell a Jammie Dodger from a custard cream, and other social faux pas, or, quicker still, simply to call them "deluded", rather than to engage with their actual arguments. Indeed, if I'm clever enough with words (and to give Dawkins credit, he can spin glittering aphorisms with a speed that would make Rumpelstiltskin[91] envious), people might not notice the trick. As Mark Twain once remarked: "A lie can get halfway around the world before the truth can even get its boots on."

I also think that the tendency to resort to insult, to *ad hominem*, says something about the state of our national public life in general – anybody who thinks we don't have a problem with civility right now simply needs to scroll to the bottom of the comments section of any online article and see

---

90   Otherwise known as string theory.
91   The little imp of fairy tale who could spin straw into gold. Much of modern banking runs on the reverse principle.

how quickly people start shouting at each other (TYPING IN CAPITALS is how you shout online, of course).[92] Such shouting at each other illustrates the biggest problem with argument-by-insult; one just trades rhetorical blows without substance. "You're *deluded*!" "You're an *idiot*!" "Religion is a mind virus!" "Science is an ersatz religion for those who are too ugly to find a partner!" – and so on. Quite frankly, my main gripe with this is not so much that it's the rhetoric of the playground, but that it's so *boring*. Pass the Jammie Dodgers, pour another cup of tea, and let's move on.

⌘

The second problem with the "God is like Santa Claus" argument concerns where Dawkins and others lay the blame for religion's failure to disappear. Whose fault is it? In a word: parents. You can put more secularism into the schools, hound God from the public square, fumigate faith from the media, but as long as parents labour under the impression that their children are their own to be raised as they wish, we have a problem. Now, given all that I've just cautioned about *ad hominem* attacks, I need to be scrupulously careful not to label the New Atheists unfairly as totalitarian control freaks on a caffeine-fuelled power trip. Much better to allow Richard Dawkins's own words to do the talking:

---

92   I grew up reading Terry Pratchett's Discworld novels, in which the character of Death always speaks IN UPPER CASE. Whenever I encounter some denizen of the Internet resorting to the same to get their point across, I always imagine Death hunched over the keyboard, banging out his points in sonorous capitals (although, given some of the spelling errors in these outbursts, especially on Twitter, you have to wonder whether it's actually the Death of Rats who looks after that side of social media). Sadly, Death and Terry Pratchett became more personally acquainted on 12 March 2015, when Terry died after a battle with Alzheimer's.

> Once, in the question time after a lecture in Dublin, I was asked what I thought about the widely publicized cases of sexual abuse by Catholic priests in Ireland. I replied that, horrible as sexual abuse no doubt was, the damage was arguably less than the long-term psychological damage inflicted by bringing the child up Catholic in the first place.[93]

That's one of those paragraphs that I had to read three times to make sure it was actually saying what I thought it was saying.[94] But apparently so: Dawkins really is claiming that a Catholic education is possibly worse than sexual abuse. So let's conduct another thought experiment. Let us imagine that, one Friday afternoon, Dawkins is sitting at home in North Oxford, composing yet another email to Sir Ian McKellen, when the telephone rings. The call is from the education department of Oxfordshire County Council and the caller apologetically explains that there's been a bit of an almighty administrative mix-up.

"I'm terribly sorry, Professor Dawkins," squawks the voice at the end of the phone, "but we lost your daughter's secondary-school application paperwork and now – well, all the schools are full …"

"All of them?" splutters Dawkins.

"I'm afraid so. Have you considered a fee-paying school? A man of your means, after all …"

"I'm against private education on principle," snaps back the professor. "I pay my taxes. I want a state-school place for my daughter."

"Well, here's the thing. We do have just two places left – not a lot of choice, I'm afraid. One is at a school run by lovely elderly

---

93 Dawkins, *The God Delusion*, p. 356.
94 A bit like airline compensation forms.

Catholic nuns, with the highest educational achievement rates in the county. The other is run by a group of sexually voracious convicted paedophiles ..."

I wonder which school Dawkins would really choose for his daughter? Worse than child abuse, indeed. Once again, we see how really bad arguments disintegrate very quickly when you turn them round and fire them back at those who wield them. Now this whole discussion would be nothing more than a fascinating rabbit trail, were it not for the fact that it's become something of an obsession for some atheists. Psychologist[95] Nicholas Humphrey, in a lecture for Amnesty International (you can't make this stuff up), produced this incredible gem:

> Children, I'll argue, have a human right not to have their minds crippled by exposure to other people's bad ideas – no matter who these other people are. Parents, correspondingly, have no god-given licence to enculturate their children in whatever ways they personally choose: no right to limit the horizons of their children's knowledge, to bring them up in an atmosphere of dogma and superstition, or to insist they follow the straight and narrow paths of their own faith. In short, children have a right not to have their minds addled by nonsense. And we as a society have a duty to protect them from it. So we should no more allow parents to teach their children to believe, for example, in the literal truth of the Bible, or that the planets rule their lives, than we should allow parents to knock their children's teeth out or lock them in a dungeon.[96]

95   Cast the word "phrenology" from your mind.
96   Nicholas Humphrey, "What Shall We Tell the Children?" in Wes Williams (ed.), *The Values of Science: Oxford Amnesty Lectures 1997*, Oxford: Westview Press, 1998, pp. 58–79 (also available online at http://www.humphrey.org.uk/papers/1998WhatShallWeTell.pdf).

One sometimes wonders whether the deepest desire of many atheists of this variety is simply that they could make parents disappear,[97] such are the hurdles they construct on the gleaming highway that leads to Progress™. Alas our genes, while possibly selfish, aren't stupid. Of course, mention of "stupid" brings us to the key idea at the heart of Humphrey's argument: children must be protected from stupidity, from "bad ideas". The problem is, who gets to decide what counts as a *bad* idea? My parents taught me many wonderful things as a child: from the importance of not running with scissors, to how to solve quadratic equations, to how to eat a chocolate éclair politely in company. And the list goes on. Just because something is taught by a parent does not automatically make it subject to suspicion. So again: *who* decides? Do parents submit a list? Should my daughter's bedtime stories be screened for appropriateness, perhaps by a government committee? Would Thomas the Tank Engine make the cut?[98] And, of course, what about bad *atheist* ideas? What about eugenics, Social Darwinism, and that ridiculous bus. Indeed, what about the Very Bad Idea implicit in Humphrey's paragraph that anybody not raising their children in a manner of which he personally approves warrants little Johnny or Jemima being taken away by the state for their own protection and re-education (but don't worry, children: Uncle Nicholas knows best).

There's a further problem, too, with Humphrey's utopian vision of wide-eyed little boys and girls, sitting in ruler-straight rows imbibing science and nothing but science, their school curricula and their homes expunged of anything that remotely

---

97   A viewpoint that many teenagers might sympathize with.
98   His constant desire to be a Really Useful Engine does seem to point to underlying self-image issues and some kind of performance anxiety. And let's not get started on the Fat Controller and eating disorders.

whiffs of religion, faith or belief. The problem is the woefully naïve idea that there is such a thing as *neutrality*, a kind of educational Switzerland of the mind,[99] a sterilized, value-free homogenous zone from which everything but pure Reason™ has been expunged. That simply doesn't work, because *values* are everywhere. For instance, the idea that Knowledge Is a Good Thing is not derived from "reason", but is in fact a *value*.[100] The belief that we should Tell the Truth in Reporting Our Scientific Results is an *ethic*. The idea that we should be Nice To One Another And Not Pull Our Schoolfriend's Pigtails is a *moral* value. The claim that we are Utterly Alone In A Godless, Purposeless, Directionless Universe In Which We Are Doomed To Oblivion is a *religious* claim, however much its advocates squeal in protest when this is pointed out. If one tries to chase out *all* religion and *all* faith from home and school, well, with it, to be consistent, go atheism and humanism and most of the school timetable.[101] You try drafting a purely "rationalistic" curriculum on which the only subjects are those that are utterly free of all subjectivity, opinion, and faith, and see how far you get: indeed, I recall that the former USSR tried a project along such lines, policing it with ruthless efficiency, and we all know how well that worked out, don't we?

So here's an idea instead: perhaps we could recognize that *everybody* has deeply held beliefs about the world (be they atheist or theist), and that most parents, most of the time, will try to raise their children in the best way they can, instilling their values in them as they do so. And guess what? There will

---

99   Although if it has chocolate, it'd be a good start.
100   Robert Spitzer, *Ten Universal Principles: A Brief Philosophy of the Life Issues*, San Francisco: Ignatius Press, 2011, pp. 5–19; 123–129.
101   See Anthony Esolen, *Ten Ways to Destroy the Imagination of Your Child*, Wilmington, DE: Intercollegiate Studies Institute, 2010.

come a time when those children will become teenagers, and teenagers will become adults, and at some point they will choose for themselves – maybe they'll even do this in a considered, balanced way, exploring the evidence for the different world views and seeing which one makes the best sense of reality. Interestingly, here those raised with some kind of religious faith have a considerable advantage. Given how secular the prevailing culture is, they will now be able to compare what they see around them with what their parents have said, and make a choice. If all a child is ever exposed to – at home, at school, and in the culture – is an insipid secularism, a lazy simply-assumed atheism that never even bothers to justify its first principles, how will they ever know there's an alternative?

⌘

One last thing. I have long been fascinated by how many people who hold a religious faith do so because they discovered it in adulthood, not because they were raised in it by their parents. Indeed, claims such as "You're only a Christian because your parents were!" have always smacked to me of desperation, on a par with "You're only pessimistic because you're English".[102] It's also an ill-tempered Rottweiler of an argument, for it can quickly turn around and bite your own hand; after all, if it were true, it would apply to atheists too. I have no idea what Dawkins's daughter, Juliet, does or does not believe – but if she is an atheist like her father, I hope she isn't having to fend off argumentative Anglicans dinging her around the head with sound bites like "You are only an atheist because your daddy is". Or maybe Dawkins displayed incredible philosophical

---

102 As James Branch Cabell quipped, the difference between a pessimist and an optimist is that an optimist believes that we live in the best of all possible worlds; a pessimist fears that this may be true.

consistency and raised her as a Mennonite, just so he couldn't be accused of foisting his beliefs on his child.

One of the questions I regularly like to ask Christian audiences is "How many of you here became a Christian after the age of fifteen?" I'm surprised by how frequently more than half the hands shoot up. But perhaps this shouldn't surprise me. As Western culture becomes increasingly secular, fewer and fewer people are being raised in religious families. That doesn't stop people finding faith. A fascinating example is Peter Hitchens: you may recognize his surname, as he is the brother of the late Christopher, the well-known atheist. Peter had the same upbringing as his brother: raised in a non-religious home, with the only religion they were exposed to coming through their schools. Like Christopher, Peter turned his back on all of this, even proudly burning his Bible when he was fifteen. He went on to become a successful journalist and found himself posted to Moscow, where first-hand experience of life under communism slowly began to erode the secular faith in politics that he had embraced as an alternative to God. Peter tells the story of his long journey to Christian faith, starting out from the same type of atheism as that of Christopher, in his book *The Rage Against God*, a book he wrote because:

> I want to explain how I became convinced, by reason and experience, of the necessity and rightness of a form of Christianity that is modest, accommodating and thoughtful — but ultimately uncompromising about its vital truth. I hope very much that by doing so I can at least cause those who consider themselves to be atheists to hesitate over their choice. I also hope to provide Christian readers with insights they can use the better to understand their unbelieving friends, and so

perhaps to sow some small seeds of doubt in the minds
of those friends.[103]

What is refreshing about Hitchens's autobiography is the raw
honesty, the degree to which he has reflected on his personal
journey – first his descent into atheism, and then his rejection
of it. He was thirty years old when he became a Christian,[104]
putting the lie to the "belief in God is like Santa" idea, as do the
stories of the hundreds of millions of people like him – such as
the tens of thousands becoming Christians every day in China,
Africa, or the Middle East, for instance. These are people for
whom faith is something they have arrived at through careful
thought and, in many cases, at tremendous personal cost.[105]

The differences between God and Santa Claus are so
obvious, really, that you wonder why any atheist ever thought
the comparison was a good one. On that I have often pondered,
and it's hard to avoid the conclusion that, when one believes
something deeply, passionately, energetically, one has a
tendency simply to grab hold of any arguments that appear
to support you, however desperate. After all, there's a chance,
isn't there, that your opponents might be right – and even
considering that is something that *some* atheists aren't willing
to permit. Better to do what fundamentalists always do – stick
your fingers in your ears and shout loudly. Perhaps sing, even;

103 Peter Hitchens, *The Rage Against God*, London: Continuum, 2010, p. 2.
104 A similar age to that at which C. S. Lewis, a notorious atheist as a young man,
became a Christian. Lewis's fascinating journey from atheism to Christianity is told in
David C. Downing, *The Most Reluctant Convert: C. S. Lewis's Journey to Faith*, Downers
Grove, IL: InterVarsity Press, 2002, or autobiographically in C. S. Lewis, *Surprised by
Joy*, London: HarperCollins, 2012 [1955]. Lewis went on to write the "Narnia" books,
putting Father Christmas into a scene in *The Lion, the Witch and the Wardrobe*, probably
deliberately to bait Richard Dawkins.
105 See e.g. Philip Jenkins, *The Next Christendom*, Oxford: Oxford University Press,
2002, and Sanneh Lamin, *Whose Religion is Christianity?: The Gospel Beyond the West*,
Grand Rapids MI: Wm. B. Eerdmans, 2003.

maybe something cheerful and heartening. So, altogether now: *"Santa Claus is coming to town ..."*

For Further Reading

Francis S. Collins, *Belief: Readings on the Reason for Faith* (New York: HarperOne, 2010)

David C. Downing, *The Most Reluctant Convert: C. S. Lewis's Journey to Faith* (Downers Grove, IL: InterVarsity Press, 2002)

Antony Flew, *There is a God: How the World's Most Notorious Atheist Changed His Mind* (New York: HarperOne, 2007)

Peter Hitchens, *The Rage Against God* (London: Continuum, 2010)

5

Aim for That Haystack!

(or: Why Psychological Arguments Against Religion Fail)

The little Cessna bounced perkily in the cloudless skies above Oxford, making us passengers feel like peas in a tumble dryer. "This is going to be fun!" my friend Dave enthused, gazing excitedly out of the window.

"*Fun?*" I asked sardonically.

"Yes! And a great way to raise money for charity, too. I love charity skydives; they put the 'fun' into '*fun*draising.'"

"Or '*fun*eral,'" I muttered under my breath. I had spent my life avoiding skydiving, feeling a natural suspicion of any sport in which progress comes more through natural selection than practice. Indeed, I still wasn't sure quite how I'd got talked into this. There'd been beer, there'd been talk of embarrassing photos from university days being released on Facebook, and then the guilt trip laid on me that, while I dithered, untold thousands were suffering. The Oxfam rep who had signed us up had grinned and said: "Think of it as win–win. If you live, you raise thousands of pounds for the starving. If it all goes badly wrong, the John Radcliffe Hospital gets your organs."

A buzzer sounded loudly in the plane, pulling me back to the present. "Time to go!" said Dave. He had skydiven[106] many times before, so we were due to perform what's called a tandem jump. Apparently, this doesn't involve plunging to your doom on a bicycle made for two, but being strapped to the front of a bearded psychopath whose first words on leaping from the plane were "Geronimo!"

The wind whistled past my ears, we spun on multiple axes several times before we levelled off, and the whole of Oxfordshire opened out beneath us. I resisted the urge to throw up. I am of the opinion that the human brain is designed to deal with geography in small chunks: this is your *village*; this is the next *farm*, etc. A concept like *this is the entire darned county* is too much for our minds to process at once.

"What a view!" shouted Dave from somewhere behind me. He glanced at his watch, one of those clever gadgets that tells you everything apart from the time. Apparently it included a vertical speed indicator.

"Look at that!" he exclaimed. "We've achieved terminal velocity."

"Have you ever reflected on how profoundly unhelpful a term that is?" I called back.

Well, the vertigo, nausea, and sheer general terror aside, the free-fall part of the jump went well. The view was, I had to admit, spectacular, and there *was* something exhilarating about flying like a bird. Even if the bird in question was one plummeting like a kakapo with concrete blocks strapped to its feet.

106 Before linguistic pedants tell me that's not a word, you try declining the verb "to skydive".

"Right," shouted Dave, "time to think about landing. I'll aim for that haystack, over there, at about two o'clock."

"I'm sorry," I yelled back. "You'll do *what*?"

"I'll aim for that haystack. Down there in that field behind the cemetery."

"I realize I'm a newcomer to this," I replied, with as much politeness as the fear and the rushing of the wind would allow, "but wouldn't, er, a *parachute* be a better option?"

"*Parachute!*" Dave spluttered back, in the same kind of tone as if I'd suggested a wet herring. "Oh, puuurrrrleeeease, you're not one of those people who believe in parachutes?"

"Well, I was kind of hoping you were too, before I strapped myself to you and leapt out of a plane."

"Parachutes are for the weak!"

"Happy to be counted among the weak," I admitted. "Eagles may soar, but weasels don't get sucked into jet engines; that's my motto."

"Why would you want a *parachute*?" Dave thundered.

"Oh, let me think now – what about this for starters: because it makes you feel better knowing you can just yank the rip cord and float down to safety …"

"I see your problem," yelled back Dave. "That's a psychological attachment you're carrying there."

"You mean my attachment to life?"

"No, no. Your view of parachutes. Parachutes clearly make you feel good, probably because you're afraid of death, or perhaps because you have fond childhood memories of seeing pictures of them, or attaching them to toy soldiers and playing with them.[107] But just because something makes you

---

107 Most of my childhood memories actually concern attempting to setting fire to things; to this day I can't see a packet of Swan Vestas™ matches without feeling a warm glow. (Which was what one of my sister's Sindy dolls felt just before it finally went whoomph.)

feel good, it doesn't make it true, does it? Now, where was that haystack ..."

⌘

Psychological arguments seem to be everywhere these days. We're told that everything – our politics and our prejudices, whom we love, what we buy, which sports team we support – can all be explained on the basis of our upbringing, our hopes and fears, our psychology. Given that psychology is so ubiquitous, it's no surprise that it has found its way into the God debate, with some atheists quick to appeal to psychology to explain away religion. Psychology, it is claimed, can explain sects as well as sex. A friend of mine tells a story of getting into a London taxi cab one Sunday after church. The driver took one look at her Bible, sneered dismissively, and then launched into a tirade against Christianity.

"Religion is a psychological crutch," he ranted. "It's something for weak, pathetic people who don't have the self-reliance, courage or strength to take responsibility for their own lives."

My friend, being English, politely responded: "Well, thank you for that."

Whereupon the driver, realizing he had probably just blown any chance of a tip, tried to recover with: "What's a nice girl like you need religion for anyway?"[108] (Or, as was once said to me by an American university student: "You're English and so you're naturally repressed and dour.[109] No wonder you choose to believe in God; it simply makes you feel good.")

The claim that religious beliefs can simply be explained

108 The story is told in Amy Orr-Ewing, *Is Believing in God Irrational?*, Downers Grove, IL: IVP, 2008, p. 43.
109 "I think you'll find that's the Scots," I tried to interrupt.

by psychology is an idea most commonly traced to Sigmund Freud, the Austrian neurologist who today is remembered as the father of psychoanalysis.[110] Along with sex, religion was a topic that fascinated Freud and, for him, it was all a psychological projection: people believe in God because they project their hopes, desires, and fears into the sky, for instance creating a heavenly version of their earthly father, somebody who is a loving and protecting guardian. We are also afraid of death and mortality, so we project the idea of heaven and an afterlife. You get the idea. This is a theme frequently returned to by contemporary atheists; for example, here is former Muslim Alom Shaha, author of *The Young Atheist's Handbook*:

> Death gives birth to gods; without death, there would be fewer gods, if any … Inventing a god is a coping strategy that has been adopted by people since prehistoric times, and it is understandable.[111]

On one level, I'd want to begin by accepting that his argument has a point. Being a thoughtful type, I do often find myself reflecting on my own mortality.[112] Now I'll be generous at this point and allow Alom a bit of a free pass on the question of why only the human animal thinks about death and needs consolation when faced with our mortality: after all, squirrels, aardvarks, and fruit bats seem to get along perfectly fine without asking themselves troubling existential questions. Thus we are

---

110 His wife also revolutionized women's undergarments with the invention of the Freudian Slip.
111 Alom Shaha, *The Young Atheist's Handbook*, London: Biteback Publishing, 2012, pp. 26–27.
112 Especially when watching *The X Factor* or when driving through Norfolk, which often causes me to ponder: "Is there more to life than Diss?"

faced with the puzzling brain-teaser of how it is that evolution, if that *is* the only game in town, has produced something quite as magnificently odd as human beings, wired to look for ultimate meaning, purpose, and comfort, even though these things are not to be found in the materialistic universe that atheists believe we inhabit. If Alom were to find himself lost in the deserts of the Arabian Empty Quarter, stumbling around desperately looking for water, his craving for hydration wouldn't mean that every sparkling glimmer on the horizon was an oasis – mirages may be more common than not. But surely his thirst should tell him that *there is such a thing as water*. So what is it, in short, that has "set eternity in the hearts of men"?[113]

But let's now turn from death to delight. It most definitely *is* the case that Christianity sometimes does make me feel good. Now I realize that admission would make Alom leap to his feet and proclaim: "Exactly! That's my very point! But Andy, just because something makes you feel good, it doesn't mean that it's true." To which I would want to respond: *precisely*. You cannot deduce whether or not something is true, or whether something exists, from how you feel about it. For instance, the thought of mint choc chip ice cream, mountain views, and sex makes me feel good.[114] So, too, does the thought of roller-skating bonsai elephants and personal teleportation devices. See the problem? You cannot use how I *feel* about something to determine its existence – there are *imaginary* things the thought of which I enjoy and there are also *real* things whose contemplation brings me pleasure. If one were to be a *consistent* psychological sceptic, one would thus have to deny not only

---

113 Ecclesiastes 3:11.
114 Not all at the same time, mind you. (The ice cream would melt on the way to the summit.)

pygmy pachyderms, but ice cream, landscapes, and sex.[115] Of course, the same point works with *negative* things too. There are many things the thought of which makes me feel fear or disgust: *Star Wars Episode I*, death, my tax return, and the Ravenous Bugblatter Beast of Traal, to name but four. But the fact that I feel *bad* about those things doesn't tell me anything about whether or not they are real. If there were an argument from the sheer awfulness of *The Phantom Menace* to the non-existence of George Lucas, I am sure that some undergraduate philosophy student and film buff would have discovered it by now.

That's all very well, I can hear potential detractors cry, but aren't you just being absurd? After all, we *know* that ice cream, mountains, sex, bad movies, and tax returns actually exist. So the comparison to God is a poor one. Well, not so fast, Socrates. Things are not nearly as straightforward as you might imagine. First, a moment's thought will remind you that we have to *trust* our minds, our consciousness, and our senses every day for our encounter with the world. You don't have first-hand experience of the ice cream: how it looks, tastes, and smells are all sensations mediated to you through your mind. Now I happen to think that our minds are, most of the time, generally reliable.[116] But it's nevertheless possible that you could be mistaken, deceived, or deluded, or that you might actually be just a brain in a jar, wired up to electrodes stimulated by a mad scientist who is simply

---

115 Although that might explain why multiple studies have shown that atheists have fewer children than religious people: see e.g. Ed West, "A nightmare for Richard Dawkins: statistics show that atheists are a dying breed", *The Telegraph*, 18 September 2009 (http://blogs.telegraph.co.uk/news/edwest/100010450/a-nightmare-for-richard-dawkins-statistics-show-that-atheists-are-a-dying-breed/). In a presentation at the Explaining Religion Conference (Bristol University 2010), Dr Michael Blume said: "We have found not a single case of a secular population retaining replacement fertility rates of more than two children per woman for a century."

116 Well, maybe not George Lucas's mind when he thought that Jar Jar Binks was a good idea.

manipulating you to conceive of the ice cream. We take more of the world on trust than we often realize. Second, there's the question of how we *interpret* reality. Consider the example of a mountain. When I stand on the summit of Kidsty Pike in the English Lake District and gaze at the vast sweep of the eastern fells, my reaction is instinctive: that is a beautiful view. But what *is* beauty? Can we measure it? Can we touch it? Is there an equation that can calculate how beautiful said view really is? Clearly not. Well then, does that mean that when I say "That's a beautiful view", I'm merely describing my personal preference, my psychology? That doesn't seem right either. Otherwise, it would be equally true to declare that the overflowing rubbish bins around the back of the local Tesco store are "beautiful", if somebody happens to think so. Beauty has to be more than mere opinion; otherwise, we're just playing word games. So if beauty isn't a material thing and it isn't a subjective, personal, psychological projection, what is it? Well, perhaps that's a discussion for another time;[117] suffice it to say that the question of existence isn't simply a case of squawking "Must see it! Must see it!" like some kind of philosophical parrot. So what about *God's* existence? Well, I'd want to suggest that there is a *wealth* of evidence that you can engage with to explore that question, ranging from philosophical and scientific arguments, to moral and ethical arguments, to arguments from literature and history, as well as those from personal experience. There are a myriad of books that cover this ground – but *this* book is not intended to be one of them.[118] My point is simply this: what you *feel* about

---

117 If you are philosophically minded, you might enjoy Roger Scruton, *Beauty*, Oxford: Oxford University Press, 2009, or C. S. Lewis, *The Abolition of Man*, New York: HarperOne, 2001 [1944].

118 You might start with N. T. Wright, *Simply Christian*, New York: HarperOne, 2006, and, if you're super-keen, progress to William Lane Craig and J. P. Moreland (editors), *The Blackwell Companion to Natural Theology*, Chichester: Wiley-Blackwell, 2009.

God doesn't answer the question of whether there *is* a God. You may *love* the idea of God, or you may *hate* the idea of God – but that simply describes your emotions and psychology and tells us nothing about his actual existence.

⌘

There are times, however, when psychology can be very helpful. Though it cannot tell us whether my belief in mint choc chip ice cream or Richard Dawkins's belief in evolution is valid, it can explore some of the reasons *why* we believe those things. Perhaps the *real* reason why I am so drawn to frozen green dairy products with chocolatey bits in them is that deep down I'm convinced that they are actually a health food.[119] Maybe the reason why Dawkins *really* believes in evolution is primarily that it annoys creationists and there's nothing he enjoys more than a hearty argument. Those examples help us to get at something quite important: it is possible to believe in things – real, existing things – for entirely wrong or incoherent reasons. Most of the time, when it comes to the "God question", I'd suggest that our deeper motives are hidden, although sometimes they surface and the person is willing to acknowledge them. I admire the candour of an atheist such as Aldous Huxley, for example:

> For myself, as, no doubt, for most of my contemporaries, the philosophy of meaninglessness was essentially an instrument of liberation. The liberation we desired was simultaneously liberation from a certain political and economic system and liberation from a certain system of morality. We objected to the morality because it interfered with our sexual freedom; we objected to the

---

119 You don't see cows suffering from cholesterol problems and cocoa is, after all, a plant.

political and economic system because it was unjust. The supporters of these systems claimed that in some way they embodied the meaning (a Christian meaning, they insisted) of the world. There was one admirably simple method of confuting these people and at the same time justifying ourselves in our political and erotic revolt: we could deny that the world had any meaning whatsoever.[120]

There's a refreshing honesty in Huxley's admission that he'd worked out that if Christianity were true, it would have some entailments – especially moral entailments – to which he was not willing to submit. Faced with that, what's a young man to do when he's full of the joys of spring with a packet of wild oats ready for sowing? Well, deny the whole thing. By claiming the world was God-free, meaning-free, and moral-free, Huxley could do entirely as he wished. But the key point is that he was led to his atheism not by the careful hand of reason but by the horny hand of lust – Huxley was a rebel, and proud of it. Other atheists who have reflected carefully on their motives have similarly admitted that their atheism is not so much rational as *emotional*; here, for instance, is philosopher Thomas Nagel:

I want atheism to be true and am made uneasy by the fact that some of the most intelligent and well-informed people I know are religious believers. It isn't just that I don't believe in God and, naturally, hope that I'm right in my belief. It's that I hope there is no God! I don't want there to be a God; I don't want the universe to be like that.[121]

---

120 Aldous Huxley, *Ends and Means: An Inquiry into the Nature of Ideals and into the Methods Employed for their Realization*, London: Chatto and Windus, 1941, p. 273.
121 Thomas Nagel, *The Last Word*, Oxford: Oxford University Press, 2001, p. 130.

A desire for personal autonomy is psychologically very understandable (anybody who has parented teenagers will know the signs instantly), but it's a perfectly bad reason to be an atheist. At the same time, let's be fair and acknowledge that both today and throughout history Christians have sometimes similarly professed faith in God for woefully bad reasons. "Because it makes me feel good" is a fine example. Even if it turned out that believing in God made you feel miserable, depressed, and nervous, even if every Bible were shipped with a packet of Prozac, that wouldn't change whether or not God is real. However, there are yet worse reasons to believe in God, I'm afraid. For instance, sometimes people have grabbed hold of religion because they have seen in it a way to achieve power, as was once pointed out by Karl Marx in this very famous paragraph:

> Religion is the sigh of the oppressed creature, the feeling of a heartless world, and the soul of soulless circumstances. It is the opium of the people.[122]

The nineteenth century was an age before the invention of modern anaesthetics[123] and so opium was widely used as a painkiller. Marx was making the point that, for the poor, this was precisely how religion functioned, alleviating their pain and distracting them from their degradation with the promise that everything would be better in the hereafter. Indeed, Marx argued, the rich elites use religion as a tool of power this very way, keeping the oppressed satiated with promises of heaven. Religion can be used as a tool of social control in other ways,

---

122   Cited in David McLellan (editor), *Karl Marx: Selected Writings*, Oxford: Oxford University Press, 2000, p. 72.
123   Or the Twilight novels, the reading of which achieves much the same effect.

too, excluding those who don't think in the right way (i.e. as *you* do) in order that you might marginalize them. Now if you're an atheist reading this, you may be nodding happily in agreement; however, there's not much breathing room to be smug. It's sobering to notice, for example, that during the eighteenth century wealthy businessmen and politicians fought to keep Christian missionaries *out* of British India, for fear they would instil in the Indians the dangerous idea that all men are equal.[124] And, a bit closer to our time, one can see how communism – the atheistic political system for which Marx helped to provide the intellectual scaffolding – became a powerful tool of exclusion: "Only *we* have the truth, because *we* are on the side of the people." And today we see a similar trend in much of the New Atheism, whose advocates love to demonize, ridicule, and marginalize those who do not think as they do.

⌘

Overall, though, appeals to psychology simply don't get us very far when it comes to questions of ultimate truth: "Christians are people who are afraid of the *dark*!" the sceptic sneers. "Atheists are people who are afraid of the *light*!" the Christian retorts. Whether or not either charge sticks is largely by the by, for neither sound bite answers the question: *which world view, atheism or theism, is actually true?* Nevertheless, there is perhaps one contribution that psychology can make here that may offer a clue. You see, it has often struck me that if Christianity *were* mere wish-fulfilment, just a psychological projection, then those who dreamt it up had pretty impoverished imaginations. Were I inventing a religion, dreaming up a deity from first principles,

---

124 See Ernest Marshall Howse, *Saints in Politics: The "Clapham Sect" and the Growth of Freedom*, London: George Allen & Unwin, 1976 [1953], pp. 65–94.

I have some pretty good hunches which direction I'd go in. Let's posit a god who is distant and doesn't interfere too much; if one must have moral commands, let's construct some that are pretty easy to keep, more along the lines of "Thou shalt not poke aardvarks with a stick" and "Thou shalt not dry thy underpants in a toaster". Let's also ensure that my à la carte religion blesses me with the freedom to spend my time and money as I wish, with no constraints. Finally, let's bolt on the promise of a low-entry-condition heaven that is full of wine, women, and song (a heaven open to all who are as *good* as me, but ideally not to those who aren't – well, you know, *decent* or who Look a Bit Funny). Were I inventing a religion out of whole cloth, I think that's what I (and I suspect most people) would shoot for. In contrast, what do we have in Christianity? A religion that demands our heart, mind, and soul: "Take up your cross," said Jesus, "and follow me." "Take up my *what*?" Either the first Christians could really have done with a couple of advertising executives and a social media consultant among the apostles, or else the sheer *difficulty*, the way that Christianity cuts against our ingrained tendency to orbit gyroscopically around our own ego, tells us something.

One of my heroes has long been the German Lutheran pastor Dietrich Bonhoeffer, arrested during the Second World War and eventually killed by the Third Reich for the stance that he took against them. Bonhoeffer had an unnerving knack for writing paragraphs that can make one feel profoundly uncomfortable, such as this one:

> If it is I who determine where God is to be found, then
> I shall always find a God who corresponds to me in
> some way, who is obliging, who is connected with my

own nature. But if God determines where he is to be found, then it will be in a place which is not immediately pleasing to my nature and which is not at all congenial to me. This place is the Cross of Christ. And whoever would find him must go to the foot of the Cross, as the Sermon on the Mount commands.[125]

Bonhoeffer is making the point that the heart of Christianity lies not in the idea that we invent, project, create, or choose God – if we did that, what we would have would be a God of our own making, one who looks suspiciously like us. (Indeed, if you are religious, a sure sign that you've done just this is that the God you claim to believe in spends most of his time benevolently blessing all of your own prejudices, desires, and ambitions). Instead, if God is really real, then we have to approach him on his own terms. I've sometimes wondered, when push comes to shoving religion off the cliff, if this is the chief problem with God for *some* atheists: he simply refuses to be domesticated. If God would simply come at my command, jump when I whistle, and keep the hell out of those areas of my life that I've clearly marked with the equivalent of "Police: Do Not Cross" tape, then it would be OK and maybe we could talk. But, of course, such a bite-sized god, whatever he might be, certainly would not be worthy of anything other than our pity and disdain. Why not just go the easier route and invest in a dachshund rather than a deity.

The late Bertrand Russell, one of the most doggedly indefatigable atheists of the last century, was once asked what he would do if he died and found himself standing before the Almighty, who demands to know why Russell did not believe in him. Russell replied that he would look God in the eye and say:

---

125 Cited in Metaxas, *Bonhoeffer*, p. 137.

"Not enough evidence, sir!" I'm often told versions of that story by sceptics, sometimes personalized in more pointed form: "If God appeared in front of me and did a miracle right here, right now, I'd believe in him instantly", I was once told by a student. Now perhaps you sympathize with this idea. If God instantly created a pink rhinoceros in your office, filled your lavatory with an angelic choir, or made the clothes of every atheist in the world instantly disappear, you'd believe. To which I'd want to ask: *Really?* Forgive me, but I think I need to call your bluff. (Or perhaps buff, if you're one of the naked atheists, shivering and trouserless.) You see, *belief* isn't really what God is looking for. As the New Testament itself memorably puts it: "Even the demons believe [in God] – and shudder!"[126] If God were to come at your whistle and perform a personal miracle, just for you, right here, right now, what precisely would you do? What would follow next: a mere reordering of your personal philosophy and the shipping of a few atheist books to the nearest charity shop? Or a life of commitment and service, the laying-down of everything – in short, the waving of the white flag and the rebel's complete surrender? Perhaps the heart of Russell's difficulty was not so much an *evidence* problem as a *commitment* problem.

Psychology fails as a weapon to attack Christianity with. But that doesn't mean that it isn't a helpful tool, reminding us (if ever we needed reminding) that human beings are, well, very human, and that we believe in things passionately and deeply for all kinds of reasons. Indeed, our motives are usually mixed and we would do well to reflect on them honestly, especially when it comes to our deepest beliefs, desires, and ambitions. One psychological problem, common to us all, is that we are, as C. S. Lewis pointed out, such "half-hearted creatures". We

---

126 James 2:19.

play around with money, sex, and power, invest so much of our time in chasing after the wind, especially in this digital age – fooling with Facebook, toying with Twitter, gazing goggle-eyed at Google – that we find it hard to lift our eyes to the bigger questions. We are too easily pleased with ephemera, like a child content to play forever with mud pies in her sandpit because she cannot conceive of what is meant by the offer of a holiday at the seaside.[127] If Christianity is *true*, it is the story of how God offers us transformative forgiveness, infinite joy, and everlasting peace – but it will cost us something: the price is our autonomy and our pride. By all means, reject Christianity because you have examined the evidence and concluded that it is false. But don't walk away because you are rebelling at a deeper level and merely hiding behind the fig leaf of bad arguments. For if your self-deceit runs *that* deep, I suggest you need something more potent than even the most skilled of psychologists can offer you.

For Further Reading

John Habgood, *Varieties of Unbelief* (London: Darton, Longman and Todd, 2000)

Malcolm Jeeves, *Minds, Brains, Souls and Gods: A Conversation on Faith, Psychology and Neuroscience* (Downers Grove, IL: IVP Academic, 2013)

Andrew Sims, *Is Faith Delusion?: Why Religion is Good For Your Health* (London: Continuum, 2011)

James S. Spiegel, *The Making of an Atheist* (Chicago: Moody Publishing, 2010)

---

127   C. S. Lewis, *The Weight of Glory*, New York: HarperCollins, 1980 [1949], p. 26.

6

Sven and the Art of Refrigerator Maintenance

(or: Why Religion Doesn't Poison Everything)

I like to consider myself somebody who is not easily surprised, but had it been physically possible, my eyebrows would probably have leapt a foot above my head on seeing the kitchen.

"Sven, what happened?" I asked, coughing from the paint fumes. No words can fully describe what my friend's kitchen looked like – it appeared for all the world as if somebody had thrown several tins of paint and a small hand grenade into the middle of it. Paint dripped from every surface, with a gentle plopping sound.

"I was trying to mend the refrigerator," Sven confessed sheepishly, fiddling with an earlobe that was also plastered with paint. In fact my Danish friend looked as if he'd just had a wrestling match with Jackson Pollock and lost.

"Trying ... to ... fix ... the ... fridge?" I repeated slowly and carefully. I scratched my head thoughtfully and was marginally disturbed to discover it was damp and sticky. I looked up to see orange paint dripping from the ceiling fan. A dozen different explanations winged their way through my mind but none seemed even remotely plausible. "Help me out here," I said after a while, "Your *fridge* was broken, so you threw *paint* around the entire kitchen?"

"Well, it's like this. I came downstairs this morning to make breakfast only to discover that the refrigerator had stopped working, along with the toaster and the waffle maker. So I poured myself a cold cup of coffee and sat down to think – "

"Kettle not working either?" I interrupted, sensing a pattern.

"Correct. So, I wondered what the common link was. And then it hit me, smack between the eyes."

"It did?"

"Yes," nodded Sven. "It was a pancake, stuck on the ceiling from last night."

"Ah," I said, wondering if Salvador Dali had also been involved in the wrestling match.

"But, as I peeled it off, I realized something."

"That breakfast at McDonald's might be a safer bet next time?" I suggested.

"No, no. I realized what all my appliances had in *common*. They were all white."

"I thought you said they weren't working."

"All *white*, not all *right*. Listen, I'm being serious."

"Sorry," I said, skilfully dodging another paint drip.

"Well, I set about repainting them. The fridge, the waffle maker, the toaster, the kettle, even my George Formby Fat-Reducing Grill."

"You mean Fore*man*."

"No, For*mby*. It plays banjo tunes while it grills. Anyway, back to the refrigerator. I repainted everything, every electrical appliance in the entire kitchen, eggshell blue, and guess what?"

"I couldn't possibly imagine," I said.

"They still didn't work. So I painted them again, forest green this time. And a third time, burnt orange. And guess what? I *still* don't have a working kitchen." Sven banged his fist on the table in frustration, causing a paint tin to crash to the floor. "*Whatever* shall I do? Do you think I am, as you English say, barking up the wrong tree?"

"Definitely barking," I agreed. "Tell me, did you try the fuse box?"

"The fuse box?" Sven slapped his forehead, leaving a perfect palm print in orange paint. "For such a little guy, you're pretty smart! I *never* thought of that."

"Well thank y – "

"I'll grab the paint and brushes; you find a flashlight. Let's head for the cellar!"

⌘

Demented though my Danish friend may have been in that, quite literally, colourful tale, Sven's basic mistake – seizing too quickly upon something that all of his ailing appliances had in common without stopping to ask himself whether it was the *right* thing in common – is a more popular error than you might think. For instance, the same basic fallacy can be spotted among one of the more popular New Atheist arguments currently doing the rounds.

Shortly after my wife and I were relocated from Oxford to Toronto in 2010,[128] the late Christopher Hitchens – then at

---

128 Either as a reward or as a punishment, we're still trying to decide.

the height of his rhetorical powers as one of the so-called Four Horsemen of the New Atheism[129] – locked horns with former prime minister Tony Blair in a debate entitled "Is Religion a Force for Good in the World?" The event was wildly popular, with tickets being touted on the streets outside for $500, making it more expensive than a Maple Leafs hockey game. By most people's analysis, Blair performed as well as the Leafs, in that he lost spectacularly. Hitchens came over as smarter, funnier, and quicker and as the king of the one-liner, notably this one: "Religion poisons everything." Wherever we look, argued Hitchens, religion is a force for ill in the world. This was a theme he had already rehearsed in his best-selling book *God Is Not Great*, which opens by listing a litany of locations where religion has gone badly wrong, including Bosnia, Belfast, Beirut, Bombay, Bethlehem, Baghdad, and the Balkans (and that's just the "Bs"). Hitchens concludes:

> As I write these words, and as you read them, people of faith are in their different ways planning your and my destruction, and the destruction of all the hard-won human attainments that I have touched upon. *Religion poisons everything.*[130]

Well, in between my own plotting how to destroy any secularists I can lay my hands on (darn that Hitchens for discovering my nefarious schemes[131]), I have read quite widely in the literary output of the New Atheists and I note that Hitchens is not the

129 Along with Richard Dawkins, Sam Harris, and Dobbin the Pantomime Horse. Sorry, I mean Daniel Dennett.

130 Hitchens, *God Is Not Great*, p. 13.

131 Shall I club the elderly atheist who lives next door over the head as he waters his tomato plants? Poison the beer at the local freethinkers' meeting at the Dog and Duck? Sprinkle anthrax into the pages of any copies of *The God Delusion* at my local library? So much destruction to cause, so little time.

only one to make this kind of accusation. Here, in similarly impassioned voice, is Sam Harris:

> Religious unreason should acquire an even greater stigma in our discourse, given that it remains among the principal causes of armed conflict in our world. Before you get to the end of this paragraph, another person will probably die because of what someone else believes about God. Perhaps it is time we demanded that our fellow human beings had better reasons for maintaining their religious differences, if such differences exist ... [T]he most monstrous crimes against humanity have invariably been inspired by unjustified belief.[132]

In the minds of many atheists, there is a veritable barrowload of guilt that can be laid at the feet of religion: war, intolerance, hatred, sectarianism, violence, dissent, tribalism, bigotry – probably even halitosis. Religion poisons *everything*. That's a powerful aphorism, eminently tweetable in its brevity, but here's the question: is it true? Well, no, not really. Indulge me, if you will, in a thought experiment. Let us imagine for a moment that because of some horrendous childhood experience in the millinery department of the John Lewis department store, I have come to believe that hats are the root of evil, the wellspring of wickedness, especially anything with a wide brim. I do some light reading,[133] engage in a little research,[134] consult widely,[135] and discover, to my horror, that the majority of the world's most evil dictators were men who wore hats. Hats also seem to be favoured by many master criminals, and you can only imagine my confirmation bias when I discover that many terrorists

---

132 Harris, *The End of Faith*, pp. 77–78.
133 Translation: search Google.
134 Translation: consult Wikipedia.
135 Translation: ask two men at the pub.

wear them, especially if one defines the term "hat" as meaning "anything that covers the head". Once you do that, it's clear that radical forms of Islam are effectively a millinerial cult. "Hats poison everything!" I proclaim to anybody who will listen, including my doctor as he patiently writes out yet another prescription for Ritalin.

A simple analogy like that one, or the tale of my paint-daubing Danish friend, should give us cause to be wary of too quickly assuming that, because we have found a common link between several phenomena, we have thereby explained them. Mao Zedong and Pol Pot had flat caps in common, an Airbus A380 and an albatross have wings in common, and Sam Harris and a walrus both have carbon atoms in common, but, in a word, *so what*? (Well, actually that's two words, but you get the point.) This whole conversation would ideally be moot, were it not for the fact that "religion poisons everything" is a remarkably tenacious idea, clinging like a limpet to the slippery rock of atheism. One of the more popular cultural expressions of it comes in John Lennon's famous song "Imagine". The music video for "Imagine" features John sitting at a piano while Yoko Ono floats around their mansion in a dressing gown, throwing back the curtains and letting light into a room painted pure white. (This was probably supposed to be a metaphor for the pure sunshine of reason flooding in and driving away superstition, but the result ends up looking more like a Dulux paint commercial. Every time I watch it, I half expect an old English sheepdog to lollop through the shot somewhere round about the third verse, its tongue lolling out goofily.[136])

---

136 For non-Brits who have not the foggiest idea what I'm talking about, see Richard Alleyne, "Power of TV – Revival of Dulux Dog adverts inspire revival in breed", *The Telegraph*, 18 February 2013 (online at http://www.telegraph.co.uk/news/uknews/9877002/Power-of-TV-Revival-of-Dulux-Dog-adverts-inspire-revival-in-breed.html).

If you recall how the song goes,[137] Lennon asks us to imagine what a world without heaven, hell or religion would look like. What a peaceful place it would be, Lennon warbles, once people have nothing left to fight or murder each other over. As "Imagine" wails to a close, Lennon admits that perhaps he's a dreamer for imagining such a utopia, but, hey, wouldn't it be amazing. What a world! Just imagine. Yet for all of his pleading, I *do* say that Lennon was a dreamer, one whose talent for chutzpah knew few bounds, not least because of "Imagine"'s other laughable cry for people to surrender their possessions and share everything. I mention this not because I'm a money-grabbing capitalist, but simply because it's a bit, pardon the pun, *rich* coming from a man who died with a net worth of more than $800 million dollars.[138] Lennon was also famous for having a violent temper, lashing out at his wife, fellow band members, and even journalists on occasions, all of which makes those lines about peace also ring a little hollow. Still, I digress. What I really wanted to question – especially given "Imagine"'s adoption as something of a secular anthem in some quarters – is that quaint suggestion that, if you simply remove religion from the equation, everybody will automatically begin living their lives in peace. Seriously? Is the suggestion *really* that if we waggled our magic wand (or perhaps Swished the Shamanistic Stick of Secularism) and made religion disappear, then instantly we would have brought about universal peace and harmony? The problem is that we've tried that experiment, several times, in history. The French Revolution represented one attempt at driving religion from society and creating a

---

137 The lyrics can easily be found on websites such as www.songlyrics.com.
138 It's also somewhat ironic that I couldn't quote "Imagine"'s actual lyrics in this book without paying hundreds of dollars per line (even the lines about no greed or possessions). Sometimes you can't make this stuff up.

secular utopia and it ended with bloody violence and the whoosh of the guillotine, including ironically for its chief architect, Maximilien Robespierre, whose Cult of Reason left tens of thousands dead. Or one might point to more recent and even grander secular re-engineering projects, such as in the former Soviet Union or in China, where a state-sponsored atheism drove out all challengers, chasing religion from society. The result? Millions upon millions dead. Imagine no religion? We don't have to *imagine*: we can simply replay the historical tape. When we do, it quickly becomes apparent that human beings have a pretty much universal tendency to try to make some finite value ultimate, to transcendentalize something – and if we exorcise Christianity from a society, into that vacuum all manner of nastiness may get sucked. Even Richard Dawkins, in one of his more magnanimous moments, remarked that "Christianity may be a bulwark against something worse".[139]

"Well, OK," I hear some atheist friends say, "perhaps atheism has its own chequered history, although I don't see how I can be held personally responsible for Mao's murderous excesses – "

"Granted," I nod. "Although wouldn't you say that making Christians feel that they're responsible for everything from the Crusades to the Spanish Inquisition is precisely how the New Atheists have often proceeded?"

"Well, most wars in history have been caused by religion ..."

This more nuanced form of the "religion poisons everything" meme is equally common. Even if religion doesn't poison everything, it poisons most things. Perhaps there's a piece of mouldy cheddar somewhere at the back of the cultural

---

139 Cited in Ruth Gledhill, "Scandal and schism leave Christians praying for a 'new Reformation'", *The Times*, 6 April 2010. (Online at http://www.thetimes.co.uk/tto/faith/article2460128.ece.)

refrigerator that hasn't been liberally sprinkled with strychnine, but religion has still proved pretty damned toxic. Look at all those wars! Well, good idea: let's do just that. There's a fascinating set of books that provides excellent bedtime reading for those of a more masochistic bent. Called the *Encyclopedia of Wars*,[140] it documents in three massive volumes some 1,763 wars between 8000 BC and AD 2003. Of these, the editors see fit to categorize only 123 conflicts as "religious".[141] That's less than 7 per cent in over ten thousand years of history – if religious types really are out to get us all, as Hitchens claims, they've got some catching up to do. Indeed, even many of that 7 per cent are probably mislabelled, since many of the wars we're quick to tag as "religious" often had secular and political goals.[142] Even today, it's easy to sloppily characterize something such as the Israeli–Palestinian conflict as a "religious" conflict when it's primarily about territory. If it were possible to magically remove all religion from the Middle East, do you imagine that all the competing land claims would instantly vanish into thin air, resulting in a Lennonesque (or even Leninesque) utopia? No, of course not. For the problem is that human beings are quick to fight about all manner of things: religion, politics, land, even farm animals (the British and the Americans almost went to war in 1859 over a pig).[143] In fact, many analysts have

140 Charles Phillips and Alan Axelrod (editors), *Encyclopedia of Wars*, Three Volumes, New York: Facts on File, 2004.

141 I owe this point to Vox Day, *The Irrational Atheist*, pp. 103–104.

142 See William T. Cavanaugh, *The Myth of Religious Violence: Secular Ideology and the Roots of Modern Conflict*, Oxford: Oxford University Press, 2009. Cavanaugh makes the helpful point (p. 4) that secular Western societies love to differentiate between *our* violence and *their* violence: "They have not yet learned to remove the dangerous influence of religion from political life. Their violence is therefore irrational and fanatical. Our violence, being secular, is rational, peace making, and sometimes regrettably necessary to contain their violence. We find ourselves obliged to bomb them into liberal democracy."

143 The so called "Pig War" was nearly triggered when an American shot a British-

suggested that a major source of armed conflict in the twenty-first century is going to be the humble H_2O molecule, as rapid population growth in water-deprived regions of the world lead to clashes. Any takers out there for "water poisons everything"?

⌘

As you gaze across the vast sweep of human history or look around the world today, it quickly becomes apparent that the basic problem with "religion poisons everything" is that it's woefully simplistic and naïve. For sure, religion can sometimes be poisonous, but so can many other things. Indeed, you could probably substitute a multitude of other nouns in place of the word "religion" in Hitchens's sound bite. Let's try this as a starter for ten: *politics*. Politics poisons everything. I grew up in Britain during the Margaret Thatcher years and, like many of my generation, I loathed the Iron Lady and everything she and the Conservative Party stood for.[144] I got involved in Labour politics, even becoming a party member for a while, and was one of millions who voted Tony Blair into power in 1997. We excitedly imagined that change would bring reform and a new kind of politics. Well, disillusionment quickly hit in the form of financial scandals, the Iraq War, and corruption, along with spin and media manipulation. *Our* lot turned out to be as bad

---

owned pig on San Juan Island, a small piece of land just east of Vancouver Island. Be thankful that the dispute was over something serious; heaven forbid the two sides had fallen out over a chicken rather than a pig: that would have been a poultry excuse.

144 Although, credit where it is due, I passed my driving test thanks to Margaret Thatcher. My test fell on the day she was forced from office and, as I arrived at the test centre, the examiner walked out of his office and asked: "Has she quit yet?" "Yes," I replied, "I just heard it on the radio – she's resigned." "Would you excuse me for one moment," the examiner said. He placed his clipboard on the roof of my car, punched the air, and shouted: "Yes! Yes! Yes!" Then he straightened his tie, retrieved his clipboard, and climbed into the car. As we drove off down the road, he was whistling. There was no way I could fail. Thank you, Margaret Thatcher.

as *their* lot. My story is not unusual: trust in politicians is at an all-time low and that's just when it comes to Western politics. Let's not start on the dog's breakfast that passes for politics in much of the rest of the world, whether its venality, violence, vice or the tendency of some communist regimes to treat their rusty political model as perfect and to break any human beings who don't fit. Politics poisons everything.

Let's try another word: what about *science*. Science, poisonous? Surely science is good and wonderful; after all, it's given us pacemakers, iPhones, space telescopes, and Bill Nye the Science Guy. Well, yes. But science has also given us thalidomide, nuclear and chemical weapons, environmental pollution, and a host of other ills. Science is far from neutral. As a salutary lesson, consider the example of Louis Frederick Fieser, one of the greatest American scientists of the twentieth century.[145] A chemist, he helped to develop artificial synthesis of vitamin K, necessary for blood coagulation, a discovery that has saved hundreds of thousands of lives. But Fieser worked on something else, too. In 1942, the US army requested his help in developing a chemical weapon that could burn tracts of jungle and eliminate troops. Fieser and his colleagues at Harvard invented napalm, a gel that sticks to human flesh when it burns. On 9 March 1945, 1,700 tons of napalm were dropped on Tokyo, burning 100,000 civilians to death. Maybe you have a strong stomach and feel that you can justify this contextually: it was the Second World War, after all, and while the roasting of children may be distressing, it does get things done. Well, things get a bit trickier when you look at how napalm was used in the Vietnam War and the

---

145 The following account is drawn from Alister McGrath, *Surprised by Meaning: Science, Faith, and How We Make Sense of Things*, Louisville, KY: Westminster John Knox Press, 2011, pp. 88–89.

indiscriminate destruction that it caused. The moral of Fieser's story is simple: for sure, science can do good. But it can also do harm, on a brutal, industrial scale: burning flesh, destroying lives, ravaging the environment. Science poisons everything, wouldn't you say?

Finally, consider *business*. Many would suggest that business poisons everything. One might point to some of its more questionable practices, such as child labour and terrible working conditions in the Far Eastern factories that build many of the glittering gadgets to which we are addicted. Then there's the corruption, nepotism, and sheer woeful incompetence that marks so much of the corporate world – look at the financial crisis that the world went through a few years back and from which we are only just recovering. Or the more thoughtful among us might point to the rampant consumerism that has our society in its grip, driven in part by business and advertising incessantly engaged in manufacturing demands, desires, and ever more exotic needs.[146] Unless you have *this* smartphone or *this* car or *this* dress, why, nobody will want to know you, you poor zeitgeist-chasing laggard. Business has caused everything to become about one thing and one thing only: the price tag.[147] Yes, I think I could make a good case that business poisons everything.

146 See the helpful pair of books by Oliver James, *Affluenza*, London: Vermilion, 2007, and *The Selfish Capitalist: Origins of Affluenza* London: Vermilion, 2008.

147 David Bentley Hart, in *The Experience of God*, makes a remarkably good case that this cultural trend helps explain the more popular forms of atheism: "It was equally inevitable that, rather than boldly challenging the orthodoxies of its age, [the New Atheism] would prove to be just one more anodyne item on sale in the shops, and would be enthusiastically fêted by a vapid media culture not especially averse to the idea that there are no ultimate values, but only final prices. In a sense, the triviality of the movement is its chief virtue. It is a diverting alternative to thinking deeply. It is a narcotic. In our time, to strike a lapidary phrase, irreligion is the opiate of the bourgeoisie, the sigh of the oppressed ego, the heart of a world filled with tantalizing toys" (p. 313).

So politics poisons everything, science poisons everything, business poisons everything. If we had the time and the inclination, we could add other items to that list: money, sex, power, journalism, goat's cheese,[148] and many more. Now hold on, I hear many people cry. Aren't I being unduly negative? (American readers may be saying to themselves, "I knew those darned Brits could be pessimistic, but it's worse than I thought. I blame their weather.") Well, no, not really. I'm not saying that there's *nothing* good to be found in any of those things I listed: business can achieve great things, science has brought us many benefits, politics when done well can solve otherwise intractable crises, and even goat's cheese has its uses, keeping mice out of the refrigerator, for instance.[149] Similarly, despite all of Hitchens's flustered fulminations, religion has done some good things too. Do a little historical delving and you'll discover from where we got the idea for one or two important things such as universities, hospitals, the modern scientific method, and human rights.[150]

However, all these things can also go wrong and go wrong *badly*. They can be used for evil as well as for good. Why? Well, to answer that, ask yourself what politics, science, business, money, sex, power, journalism, and religion (let's leave the goat's cheese behind for now, ideally some distance away and downwind) have in common. Well, for one thing they're all nouns. They're *words*. And words don't really do anything.

---

148 The stuff tastes like goats smell, for goodness' sake. Personally, I think that any goat even found in possession of cheese-making equipment should be arrested and made into curry.

149 There are some things that even vermin won't eat.

150 See e.g. James Hannam, *God's Philosophers: How the Medieval World Laid the Foundations of Modern Science*, London: Icon, 2009; Thomas E. Woods, *How the Catholic Church Built Western Civilization*, Washington, DC: Regnery Publishing, 2005; Thomas Cahill, *How the Irish Saved Civilization: The Untold Story of Ireland's Heroic Role from the Fall of Rome to the Rise of Medieval Europe*, New York: Anchor, 1995.

Nobody has been ambushed by an adjective, vanquished by a verb, or clobbered by a conjunction. Words sit there inertly in the dictionary and thesaurus, minding their own business until a human being picks them up and does something with them. You see, it is *human beings* that are the common link and, more specifically, it is the involvement of human beings that explains why all these things can be used for good or for ill, to harm or to heal. For we seem to be peculiarly divided creatures, able to grasp all manner of things, from religion to science, and use them for great good, or to use them for great evil. What explains this? The Russian novelist Aleksandr Solzhenitsyn gets as close to the mark as any thinker. Imprisoned and tortured as he was by the Soviets for his dissenting political views, one would have thought that Solzhenitsyn, more than most people, would have been quick to cry "Politics poisons everything" and to denounce his captors as uniquely evil. But he was far wiser than that and instead wrote these words: "The line between good and evil passes not through states, nor between classes, nor between political parties either, but right through the middle of every human heart and through all human hearts."[151] In other words, it is *we* who poison everything. Christianity has a name for this split, this fracture, this riven quality to the human condition: it calls it original sin, or fallenness.[152] Now before my sceptical readers chortle into their cappuccinos, giving themselves funny little milk moustaches in the process, I would point out that an atheist of no less a stature than John Gray, former Professor of European Thought at the London School of Economics and certainly no fan of religion, has something very interesting to say in his book *Heresies*:

151 Aleksandr Solzhenitsyn, *The Gulag Archipelago: 1918–1956*, New York: HarperCollins, 2002, p. 75.
152 See Alan Jacobs, *Original Sin: A Cultural History*, London: SPCK, 2008.

> Liberal humanism is a secular rendition of a Christian myth, but the truth in the myth has been lost on the way. The biblical story of the Fall teaches that evil cannot be rooted out from human life. Humans are radically flawed – a perception rooted in the doctrine of Original Sin. It is not error or ignorance that stands in the way of a better world. The human animal may yearn for peace and freedom, but it is no less fond of war and tyranny. No scientific advance can answer the contradictions of human needs. On the contrary, they can only be intensified as science increases human power.[153]

This is profoundly uncomfortable, because deep down most of us are pretty wedded to the idea that we're basically good.[154] That if we were to divide the world into "good" and "bad" people, we would, contra Solzhenitsyn, stand on the sideline with the good guys. I haven't killed anybody, or started a land war in Europe, or exploited the poor, or sold goat's cheese, or done any of those other poisonous things. Well, nice try, but no dice. You are, if you're honest with yourself, basically a pretty mixed bag, as am I. All too quickly I can be cruel as well as kind; mean as well as munificent; as quick to hold a grudge as to forgive; petty and spiteful as well as generous; compassionate one moment, the very next willing to rejoice when somebody else fails. The same goes for you. You are, like me, part of that marvellously diverse and complex tribe, the human race, and collective responsibility catches us all up, no matter how fast we try to outrun it. *"I didn't exploit the poor!"* Well, no, but you have enjoyed cheap food, clothing, and gadgetry made possible by unconscionably low wages. *"I haven't polluted the environment!"* Again, maybe not

---

153   John Gray, *Heresies: Against Progress and Other Illusions*, London: Granta, 2004, p. 8.
154   In the same way that most people think they are better-than-average drivers, even after they've bounced the Honda off a lamp post for the third time.

personally, but tell me with a straight face that your lifestyle hasn't contributed to its pillaging. *"I'm an atheist, so don't blame me for the evils of religion!"* Well, nice to see you here, Professor Dawkins, but I'm afraid things aren't that simple: if atheism is true, then religion is a wholly *human* invention and there's no god at whose door we can lay the blame. Religion simply shows, on your view of the world, just how utterly irrational humans can be: in which case, could you perchance explain precisely why we should trust you and the rest of the New Atheist Illuminati to run the world on enlightened secular principles?

Wherever Solzhenitsyn's line is drawn, at times you and I – and Richard Dawkins – find ourselves falling on one side of it or the other. This is, of course, entirely what one would expect, if Solzhenitsyn was correct about its running right through the middle of our heart. Now maybe this is depressing or disheartening – or perhaps, if you're like me, you may see it as a refreshing blast of invigorating cool air. The doctor's diagnosis may come as a bombshell, but once the shock has passed, at least we now know where we stand. Indeed, perhaps the news can even be seen as liberating and releasing, for it can be so damn *wearying* trying to keep ourselves moving fast enough that we don't have time to notice our cracks, flaws, and twistedness. Keep yourself busy, bury the questions, hope that music, or movies, or Google's glowing allure can distract you from noticing the problem. It's equally tiring trying to go one further, persuading yourself on a daily basis that you're basically a Jolly Good Person and that everybody else is the problem. I pity my poor New Atheist friends, hauling themselves up the sheer cliff face of their Moral Mount Sinai each morning so that they can stand on the summit and hurl stones at the poor religious fools in the valley below. That's exhausting, quite frankly.

Others, however, are a bit wiser. A few years ago, the Canadian novelist Douglas Coupland wrote an autobiographical novel which explored the way that his generation (he grew up in the 1960s) tried to throw out religion and tackle all these questions under their own secular steam. Listen to what he says:

> Now – here is my secret: I tell it to you with an openness of heart that I doubt I shall ever achieve again, so I pray you are in a quiet room as you hear these words. My secret is that I need God – that I am sick and can no longer make it alone. I need God to help me give, because I no longer seem capable of giving; to help me to be kind, as I no longer seem capable of kindness; to help me love, as I seem beyond being able to love.[155]

Now this is the point at which, if you are of a sceptical persuasion, you may very well be thinking "Here comes the bait and switch", rather like that moment when it dawns on you that the free food and wine have run out and you've now got to sit through a two-hour presentation on the wonders of timeshare ownership in the Algarve. Wait for it, any moment now, Andy's going to launch into "Human beings are a crazy, mixed-up, broken bunch, but, hey, Jesus is the answer". Well, as a Christian, I happen to think that he is. But how's this for a suggestion: maybe we need to identify the *questions* before we leap headlong into the answer. This is, incidentally, precisely the problem with much of the New Atheist literature. We've barely read as far as the bottom of the very first page of Dawkins's preface before we're being told in glowing, evangelical terms that atheism can make a person happy, balanced, moral, and intellectually fulfilled. (Oh, and modest too.) "Atheism is the

---

155   Douglas Coupland, *Life After God*, New York: Pocket Books, 1995, p. 359.

answer!" Dawkins cries. Thanks for that, Richard. Now, what precisely was the *question* again?

A few months ago, I met a young university student who introduced himself to me as an agnostic. "I used to be a Christian," he went on to explain, "but I was raised in a fundamentalist family. Any critical questions about religion were forbidden, as they were at my church. If you ever challenged anything, you were told that asking questions like that would send you to hell. So I began reading atheist books and, lo and behold, one thing led to another and I abandoned my faith. I could finally see religion for what it was: dangerous, irrational, and oppressive."

"But you introduced yourself as an 'agnostic'," I said gently. "What happened?"

"I started attending a local atheist group," he replied, "in which half the members turned out to be former Christians like me, along with a smattering of other iconoclastic types. And I quickly discovered something." He leaned in closer and whispered conspiratorially: "They're all fundamentalists too. Everything was black and white, everything was certain; if you dared to question anything written by one of their favourite authors, you'd get shouted down. There were also power struggles and politics – all the things I'd seen and hated in the church."

"So ... now what?" I asked.

"I don't know *what* I believe or disbelieve any more. I guess that's why I've settled on the term 'agnostic'. Do you think that's lazy?"

"Well, there are two types of agnostic," I replied. "You can be a *lazy* agnostic, yes – which I'd define as somebody who can't be bothered to find the answer to the God question. Alternatively, you can be an *active* agnostic – somebody who is genuinely searching for the answer but just hasn't found it yet."

We talked for a long time that evening but I left the young man with this thought: religion *can* be poisonous, and fundamentalism, of all kinds, can do incredible damage. But here's what fascinates me: first, if atheists of all people are going to critique Christianity on this score, they would do well to note from where they're picking up the sticks to beat us with. You see, if atheism is true, then religion is purely a human invention and, like all human creations, it can harm as well as help. So just live with it and let natural selection, that most powerful of sieves, strain out the adaptations that work from those that do not. If Mother Nature approves of the evolutionary benefits of religion, well we're stuck with it, like it or not. On the other hand, if the values wired so deeply into Christianity are *true*, then it is meet and right to hold Christians to account when we fall short of them. Which leads to a second point: critiquing bad religion is not something that Christopher Hitchens first dreamt up as he sat down at his word processor one evening to bang out *God Is Not Great*. That religion sometimes can go badly wrong is a much older point, indeed one made some 2,000 years earlier by Jesus himself. His most frequent clashes were with the religious leaders of his day, whom he accused of using religion for personal gain, or as a tool to exploit and to marginalize. In short, if you're going to criticize religion when it goes wrong, you're possibly closer to Jesus on that issue than you might ever have imagined.

For Further Reading

Bruxy Cavey, *The End of Religion: Encountering the Subversive Spirituality of Jesus* (Colorado Springs, CO: NavPress, 2007)

Ross Douthat, *Bad Religion: How We Became a Nation of Heretics* (New York: Free Press, 2012)

Timothy Keller, *The Prodigal God: Recovering the Heart of the Christian Faith* (London: Hodder & Stoughton, 2009)

Douglas Wilson, *God Is. How Christianity Explains Everything: A Reply to Christopher Hitchens' "God Is Not Great: How Religion Poisons Everything"* (Powder Springs, GA: American Vision Press, 2008)

7

The Lunatic in the Louvre

(or: Why Science Cannot Explain the Entirety of Reality)

Ah, Paris in the springtime. The smell of the food, the glitter of the sun on the Seine, the terrified screams of tourists almost mown down by taxi drivers racing up the Champs-Élysées. I've always loved Paris, and so when Claude, an old schoolfriend, contacted me on Facebook and invited me to visit next time business took me to France, I thought I would seize the opportunity. Claude kindly picked me up from the Eurostar Terminal at Gare du Nord in his battered old Citroen.

"Have you seen the Louvre before?" he asked. "It's one of the highlights of our city."

Well, the museum was everything I'd anticipated and more. We gazed at the Winged Victory of Samothrace, ogled the Code of Hammurabi, and contemplated the Seated Scribe.

"The sculpture is over 4,500 years old! Dug out of the ground in 1850 in Saqqara in Egypt by an archaeologist called Auguste Mariette – a *Frenchman*," Claude said proudly. We turned to see a gaggle of Japanese tourists, cameras in hand, standing behind us and listening intently. "Sorry," said Claude, "I'm not a tour guide. That's the sum total of my knowledge." Their group leader smiled and bowed but didn't move. "Let's escape to the cafeteria," Claude whispered.

The museum café was quiet and calming and the food excellent, but the wine – the moment I took the first sip I realized something wasn't quite right. I felt light-headed and the room began slowly to spin. The last thing I remember is muttering something about needing some air, standing up in a wobbly manner, and then everything went black.

I came round with a start. Everything was still black. I sat up slowly, nursing a migraine that felt as if a troupe of hippopotami were dancing a jig somewhere in my skull. As my eyes grew accustomed to the darkness, I saw that I seemed to be lying on the floor behind what appeared to be a large pot plant. "My head hurts," I groaned. "What the hell happened?"

A flashlight clicked on and illuminated Claude's face, grinning like a close relative of the Cheshire Cat. "The headache will pass," he whispered. "It's a common side effect of *Vin de Diazepam.*"

"Diazep – what the hell! You *drugged* me! Are you mad? Where are we?"

"Where we were before – in the Louvre!"

The torch threw just enough light for me to see my watch. "The Louvre? But it's gone midnight," I protested.

"Exactly," hissed Claude. "The guards will all be sleeping like babies by now." He indicated with his thumb to where one was slumped over a display case, snoring loudly.

"Sleeping?"

"Diazepam," he nodded sagely. "Now – to business." From

behind another potted plant, Claude produced a large silver flight case.

"How the hell did you get that in here?"

"It's amazing what you can get away with if you walk confidently and carry a clipboard. Now, follow me."

In a daze, I staggered along behind Claude as we walked down hallways, stepping over prone security guards, through a gift shop, up staircases, and through a cupboard that I swear contained half of a stuffed rhinoceros, before finally emerging in a gallery I recognized. We'd visited it earlier that afternoon, in fact, when I was a mere tourist, rather than the unwitting accessory to what was looking increasingly like an art heist.[156] There, on the wall, the pride of the Louvre hung in all her glory: Leonardo da Vinci's *Mona Lisa*. It was smaller in real life than you'd imagine from the photographs, but then people say that about me.

"Won't she be alarmed?" I hissed.

"I'd describe her expression more as 'nonplussed,'" Claude grinned.

"You can't *possibly* get away with stealing the *Mona Lisa*," I protested. "I know the French gendarmerie are not the quickest in the world, but somebody will notice. What do you plan to do with her anyway? Sell her on eBay?"

"Steal her?" exclaimed Claude. "That would be a *crazy* idea. I'm not a lunatic, you know."

"Well, that's a relief. What with the drugging people and the sneaking around art galleries after dark, I *was* beginning to wonder."

"No, no," he said. "I just plan to cut away some of the frame, so I can remove some paint samples. I also want to cut off some pieces

---

156 I was convinced Claude was in it for the Monet.

of the wood panel she's painted on – that's all. Perfectly harmless." Claude flung open the flight case and the torchlight glimmered on a collection of knives, chisels, saws, and a hand-drill.

The soothing effect of the drugs was beginning to wear off and now the panic began to rise. "Are you *insane*? We'll get twenty years! This is the *Mona Lisa*, not *The Fallen Madonna with the* – "

"Insane?" exclaimed Claude, looking genuinely offended. "This is *research*."

"Research?"

"Yes. Have you never wondered *why* Leonardo painted Lisa del Giocondo with that curiously enigmatic smile."

"I always thought she was suffering from constipation – "

"Funny, my little English friend, funny."

"Well, OK, I guess I occasionally wondered. But that's never led me to loot the Louvre. Why can't you just Google the answer, like a normal person?"

"I'm a *scientist*!" exclaimed Claude. "If I wanted simply to slavishly copy the opinions of others, I'd have become a journalist. No, once I have a little paint, I can run a spectrographic analysis, and once I have a sample of the wood, I can do a little dendrochronology."

"Isn't he the actor who starred in *Safe House*?"

"That's Denzel Washington. Dendrochronology is the study of tree-ring dating. You can use it to date a piece of wood."

"Don't you think that somebody is going to notice the *Mona Lisa* has holes in it?"

"Nobody noticed when I borrowed one of the Venus di Milo's arms using an angle grinder. Now, pass me that handsaw … "

⌘

At first glance, it would seem that the most obvious conclusion to draw from Claude's hare-brained scheme is that he was completely, entirely, and utterly mad. Who could possibly imagine that the way to answer a question of art history (the reason why Leonardo painted the *Mona Lisa* in the style that he did) could be answered by analysing the paint's chemical composition or studying the wood frame? However hard you try, however much energy you expend, no matter how deep your pockets or endless your supply of Diazepam, you are simply not going to answer such a question using science. Thus Claude must be some kind of lunatic, for otherwise from where could he have got the idea that science can answer *any* question?

Well, maybe from a statement like this: "Science is the only philosophical construct we have to determine truth with any degree of reliability."[157] That pronouncement was made by Harry Kroto, a man who is no dribbling village idiot but rather a Nobel-Prize-winning chemist. The technical term for Harry's idea is *scientism*, the view that science can answer any and all questions, that it can quite literally encompass the whole of reality, from the secrets of supernovae to the laws of cricket. Now Kroto is not alone in this view. For example, Richard Dawkins claims that "scientists [are] the specialists in discovering what is true about the world and the universe",[158] while one of the greatest physicists of recent decades, Stephen Hawking, wrote:

> [P]hilosophy is dead. Philosophy has not kept up with modern developments in science, particularly physics.

157 Cited by P. Z. Myers at http://scienceblogs.com/pharyngula/2011/07/theres_something_obvious_missi.php. The original quote can be found in *The Times*, 7 April 2011.
158 Richard Dawkins, *A Devil's Chaplain: Selected Writings*, London: Phoenix, 2004, p. 242.

> Scientists have become the bearers of the torch of discovery in our quest for knowledge.[159]

I was recently involved in filming a TV documentary exploring this very question and got to interview another leading atheist, the chemist Peter Atkins. We had a fun couple of hours together during which we disagreed about almost everything; I was particularly struck by something Peter said when I asked him about the explanatory power of science. Very excitedly, he announced:

> Humanity should be proud that he [sic] has actually stumbled into this way of understanding the world and that it really can attack every problem that concerns humanity with the prospect of an outcome. Science also gives you the promise of understanding while you're alive, whilst religion offers the prospect of understanding when you are dead.[160]

On many levels, I can understand why science has been elevated to religion-like status, so much so that other disciplines have come all over self-conscious and feel they can't justify themselves unless they stick "science" in there somewhere – Computer Science, Social Science, Sports Science.[161] After all, science is so twenty-first century, so hip, so *now*: it has graphs, statistics, flashing lights, and Sheldon Cooper. It also attracts

---

159 Cited in Stephen Hawking and Leonard Mlodinow, *The Grand Design*, New York: Bantam Books, 2010, p. 5.
160 Peter Atkins, *Burning Questions* TV documentary, Episode 2: "God and Science" (http://www.burningquestions.ca). I resisted the temptation to point out that, especially in chemistry, scientists who are not too careful may actually end up combining understanding with death. "Is this hydrogen? Is this a naked flame? Why, I do believe th – " BANG!
161 There's a great discussion of this trend in chapter one of Ian Hutchinson, *Monopolizing Knowledge*, Belmont, MA: Fias Publishing, 2011.

huge amounts of funding, and, of course, even a gibbon looks intelligent if you stick him in a lab coat and give him a pair of spectacles. The message of the media seems to be that if a scientist says it, it must be true – right? Well, that rather depends on *what* they're saying: I want to suggest that if the scientist in question is opining, in a manner that suggests they expect you to take them seriously and this isn't some kind of April Fool's Day prank, that Science Can Explain Everything, well we need to point a few things out.

The first is that it's *wrong*. Not just *slightly* wrong, in the way that how Americans make tea is wrong. Not even *significantly* wrong, in the way that any tweet by Richard Dawkins that contains the words "rape" or "Down's Syndrome" is wrong.[162] But completely, entirely, utterly, Hindenburgesquely wrong. We already saw a hint of the problem during our Louvrean adventure, but let's illustrate it again from a different direction. Consider the question: what is the value of a human life? Now that's not a question merely plucked at random from the ether, but is arguably one of the most important questions of all – the answer to it lies at the root of ethics, law, and justice. So let's proceed and try to imagine how one might answer it using science alone. Now, were I a biologist or a chemist, I might answer the question in terms of the value of the molecules that make up your body: you consist of so much iron, potassium, carbon, water, and so forth. I could even drug you while you sleep and drag you off to my secret laboratory buried deep beneath Chipping Norton,[163] where I could boil you down to

162 See Lizzie Deardon, "Richard Dawkins tweets: 'Date rape is bad, stranger rape is worse'", *The Independent*, 29 July 2014 (http://www.independent.co.uk/news/people/richard-dawkins-says-date-rape-is-bad-stranger-rape-is-worse-on-twitter-9634572.html) and "Richard Dawkins apologises for causing storm with Down's syndrome tweet", *The Guardian*, 21 August 2014 (http://www.theguardian.com/science/2014/aug/21/richard-dawkins-apologises-downs-syndrome-tweet).
163 Property prices for secret lairs in more exotic locations have skyrocketed of late.

your chemical parts, advertise them on eBay, and see what bids I received. Not a very promising approach, I admit, so perhaps we should try the soft rather than the hard sciences. Were I an economist,[164] perhaps I'd want to look at what you can produce, at your net contribution to the economy. I could even lock you in a shed with a whittling knife and an endless supply of sticks and see how many Justin Bieber Bobbleheads you could knock out in a year. Or maybe if I were a sociologist, I could look at your value to the community. I could count how many friends you have (both the *real* kind and the you've-only-ever-met-through-Facebook kind). I might hold you to ransom and see how much your friends and relations would be willing to cough up to release you. All these and more would be ways of trying to ascertain what you're worth. Some would get me arrested or sectioned, but none would actually answer the question. Indeed, we all know – instantly, instinctively, inherently – that these are not merely wrong but are terrible ways to value a human life. Your value is not derived from your chemical constituents, your relationships, or your production. If we go down that route, we're all in trouble (unless you're a grossly overweight lawyer with great social networking skills). Rather, most of us would want to say that human beings have *intrinsic* value, yet, no matter how much "science" you do, you won't derive that answer. Science may be able to comment on what you're *made of*; what it can't determine is what you *are* – and there's a huge difference. This book, for instance, is made of paper and ink;[165] the *Mona Lisa* is made of wood and pigment; a human being is made of atoms. But that's not what a book, a

---

164 An economist is somebody who will be able to tell you tomorrow why the prediction they made yesterday turned out to be wrong today.

165 Unless you've got one of those new-fangled e-book things. Until you can beat wasps to death with a Kindle, I'm sticking with the old technology.

painting or a person *is*. You know this, I know this, and even Richard Dawkins knows this: when he rages against religion, he clearly thinks it is *people* he is furious at. However, if his narrow, science-only view of reality holds, getting annoyed with a person is simply being irritated with a sack of chemicals. If he were being consistent, Dawkins might as well vent his anger at radishes, sofas, duffle coats or, for that matter, the humble carbon atom. People, in the sense of being *persons*, don't really exist if scientism is true. But if it's any consolation, neither does Richard Dawkins.

"Well maybe I don't care about the value of human life," says the chemist. "Maybe I'm a closet sociopath; indeed, maybe the reason I went into a field in which I spend much of my time smelling distressingly of hydrogen sulphide, with suspicious stains on my lab coat and scorch marks in my mad hair,[166] is that I don't want anything to do with people. Don't try to confuse me with your appeals to compassion, morality, and human dignity." OK, well in that case let me instead point out something closer to home, namely how a claim such as "science is the only reliable way to uncover truth" actually destroys science itself. How? Well, consider one of the major pillars on which science rests, the idea that knowledge is a good thing. Here's Christopher Hitchens in full rhetorical flow:

> [W]e are in need of a renewed Enlightenment , which will base itself on the proposition that the proper study of mankind is man, and woman ... The pursuit of unfettered scientific inquiry, and the availability of new findings to masses of people by easy electronic means, will revolutionize our concepts of research and

---

166 Tell me you couldn't have guessed Einstein's profession from his hairstyle if you didn't already know.

> development ... And all this and more is, for the first
> time in our history, within the reach if not the grasp of
> everyone.[167]

What a vision! Who couldn't possibly want unfettered scientific enquiry with a side order of Enlightenment sauce, served up fresh to the masses every day? But hang on just a moment, Christopher, there's a hand at the back. OK, speak up, young man. "Why is the pursuit of knowledge a good thing?" Well, what a good question. Christopher? *Christopher*? Oh dear, he appears to have nipped out for a quick drink. And I don't blame him, because it's a phenomenally tricky question and one that many atheists often overlook: *why* is the gaining of scientific knowledge a good thing? You might just possibly be able to answer that question when it comes to research that dramatically advances the quality of life, perhaps a breakthrough in medicine that discovers the cure for folk music appreciation, or in food technology that unlocks a wondrous new flavour of ice cream. But what about when it comes to some of the more arcane areas of research. Do we really need to know why onions make people cry? Or whether it would be possible to run across a pond on the moon? Or that chimpanzees can recognize another chimpanzee purely by seeing a picture of their bottom?[168] After all, if we're just a collection of chemicals, sloshing around in our protoplasmic sacks, fizzing away, why bother? Why does it matter? What is it about the gaining of knowledge that could reduce a grown man like Christopher Hitchens to misty-eyed romanticism? In other words: why expend any effort on doing science at all? Why not cut all government funding for the

---

167 Hitchens, *God Is Not Great*, p. 283.
168 All these were examples of Ig Nobel winners, a prize awarded each year to scientists engaged in the most imaginative or unusual research projects.

sciences and burn the lot on one tremendously wild, really exciting party? (We'd even invite the nerds.) In short: what is it about science and the pursuit of knowledge that is so darned special? I put it to you that this is not a question that science can answer for us.

Not merely is there the question of *why* science exists;[169] there's also the question of *how* science works. Science stands not merely on foundational ideas about the value of knowledge; it is also built on the ethic that telling the truth and reporting your results accurately are good things. It's not considered sporting to lie, cheat or make up results for your article in *Nature* or *Scientific American* – although we can't always trust individual scientists to toe the line on this one, which is why peer review and sodium pentothal were invented. But we can again ask *why*? Why is it wrong to lie about your results? Perhaps huge amounts of money are riding on your laboratory making some new discovery before your rivals, those dastardly scoundrels at Fen Bog College down the road. What does it matter if you – well, you know, *fudge* the figures slightly. Tweak a chart there, misreport a statistic here, bury a failed experiment behind the privet bushes there. After all, nobody is harmed in the long run. Now put this suggestion to most scientists and steam often issues at high pressure from both their ears – ethics is taken very seriously in science. But the problem is that you can't derive ethics *from* science. No matter how many experiments you run, you will not produce "Do Not Lie About Your Results" in a test tube or a particle accelerator.

Now sometimes when I've made this point to science aficionados, the response has been "We don't need to worry about trusting scientists, because science is *repeatable*". In other

---

169   As a thirteen-year-old boy, I'd have said that the answer was Carol Vorderman.

words, if I don't trust the results of a particular scientist, I can go out and try to repeat them. It's often claimed that this virtue of repeatability lies at the very heart of the scientific method. The problem, of course, is that it's not quite true. Consider the Large Hadron Collider at CERN in Switzerland, one of the largest scientific instruments every made, built to smash atoms into each other at high speed in an attempt to unlock the secrets of subatomic particles (and possibly to create new flavours of Maltesers). Now, let's imagine that I am of a sceptical persuasion and I become suspicious of claims that physicists have used the Collider to discover the famed Higgs boson particle. "Repeatability!" I exclaim. No, I'm not going to take this at face value; what I want to do is to recreate their results for myself. There's just one itsy-bitsy little problem: the small matter of planning permission to dig a seventeen-mile-long tunnel starting in my back garden and the minor question of where I can find six billion dollars in funding. Perhaps, on second thoughts, I ought to take it on trust after all. Thank goodness, then, that those scientists are such ethical chaps!

⌘

The moral of all of this is that science is a wonderful tool, a powerful tool, possibly the best tool that humankind has ever invented,[170] but it is only *one* tool and, like any tool, there are places where it works well and there are others where it simply doesn't work at all. Try painting a portrait with a shovel or performing dentistry with a pickaxe and you'll see what I mean. The problem, though, is that some popular atheist writers typify the old proverb: "To the man who only has a hammer,

170 Apart from the toothpick. Sure, physics is great, but you try modelling the event horizon of a black hole with a raspberry pip stuck between your molars and see how far you get.

everything looks like a nail." It's tempting to add that, in the case of Dawkins and many of his fellow New Atheists, they have also taken the rest of the tools and buried them in a field, which they've then sown with landmines. Oh, and they've burned all the books that mention other tools. "Needle-nosed pliers? Sorry, mate, never heard of those. But here, have a hammer." Human nature? Bang! Philosophy? Wallop! Religion? Whack-whacketedy-thwack! Of course, if you wield a hammer with too much carefree joie de vivre you're going to strike a few thumbs in the process, not to mention that if your goal is, say, a set of shelves fully built and finished, your hope might extend beyond the humble hammer to a saw, drill, screwdrivers, and even a paintbrush or two. And just as you need the whole toolbox if you're going to get the DIY job done correctly, so we need more tools in our philosophical toolkit than just science if we're going to answer all the wonderfully rich and varied questions that are out there to be explored.

In particular, many of life's deepest questions require multiple levels of explanation. Let me illustrate what I mean. When I am not speaking or writing, one of my hobbies is climbing mountains, and my favourite place to indulge in this pursuit is the Lake District. Imagine that you were to meet me, one sunny afternoon on the top of Kidsty Pike, a rocky protuberance on the eastern fringes of Lakeland. "I'm keen to know why you've climbed this mountain!" you announce, but, before I can reply, you whip off your rucksack and from its cavernous interior produce a veritable cornucopia of scientific gadgetry with which you measure my heart rate, blood pressure, oxygen capacity, blood-sugar level, and so forth. Finally you produce a hammer from the depths of your rucksack: "I just need to test your reflexes," you explain. Well, we're back in Louvre

Land again, for all of those tests, fascinating as their results no doubt are, wouldn't really help us. For sure, one answer to the question "Why did Andy climb Kidsty Pike?" is "Because his cardiovascular system was in good working order". But, like a microwave Chinese meal for one, that doesn't fully satisfy, does it? Your tests would not have revealed that I spend most of my spare holidays in the Lake District. Nor would they have uncovered the fact that I am geekily working through the list of 214 Lake District summits compiled by the great fellwalker Alfred Wainwright, ticking them off as I go. No test would have revealed my appreciation of the beauty and history of this part of England, nor my appreciation of the Romantic poets, such as Wordsworth and Coleridge, who tramped these peaks and were inspired by the views. In order to discover that, you would need something more than science, something other than a hammer. You would need to ask me.

But by asking me you have moved from the realm of science to the realm of revelation, as you would have asked me to *reveal* my answer. Now at this point I can imagine red warning lights flashing and klaxons going off in the minds of some people. I find that many atheists get worked up very quickly about the "r word". Rhubarb? No, not that word. *Revelation*. Isn't the whole purpose of science to draw a line of demarcation, hundreds of feet deep and ringed with barbed wire and tank traps, in order to keep anything that even smells of theology out of the discussion? Geneticist and atheist Richard Lewontin admits as such:

> It is not that the methods and institutions of science somehow compel us to accept a material explanation of the phenomenal world, but, on the contrary, that we are forced by our *a priori* adherence to material causes

to create an apparatus of investigation and a set of concepts that produce material explanations, no matter how counter-intuitive, no matter how mystifying to the uninitiated. Moreover, that materialism is an absolute, for we cannot allow a Divine Foot in the door.[171]

That's quite a statement. What Lewontin is saying is that scientists cannot, will not, must not allow room for anything other than purely scientific, purely materialistic explanations, because to do so would run the risk that God might get a look in. But of course his claim goes much further than that: if the only explanations that are allowed are those that are material, not only does divine agency go winging out of the window, but so does something else, namely reason itself. Let me explain why. First, think back to my mountain-climbing example. Imagine that you were to lay aside your battery of instruments for a moment – perhaps it has rained and they are sodden, or, miraculously, the sun has come out but that has melted your chocolate-coated Kendal Mint Cake and ruined everything in your rucksack. Never mind, let's try the old-fashioned way: you *ask* me to give you my reasons. Well, if Lewontin is right, you have now crossed the bridge to the Land of Lunacy, because you have moved beyond material causes to look for personal ones. But guess what? You can *test* what I say to you. I claim I frequently holiday in the Lake District, so check my bank account: if, every summer, my credit card statements show numerous purchases of sandwiches in Keswick, then perhaps I am telling the truth. You might rummage through my bookcases, find my battered collection of Wainwrights,[172] and note how I have ticked off and

171 Richard Lewontin, "Billions and Billions of Demons: A Review of Carl Sagan's 'The Demon-Haunted World: Science as a Candle in the Dark'", *New York Review of Books*, 9 January 1997.

172 A. Wainwright, *A Pictorial Guide to the Lakeland Fells*, Seven Volumes, London:

dated each summit. Some pages even have rain marks and what look worryingly like sheep poo stains, but there you are. Finally, you flick through my photo collection and discover thousands of photographs of the mountains.[173] All of this is *evidence* that the information I have *revealed* to you is true. In short, revelation is not contrary to reason.

But *scientism*, the idea that science can tell us everything, is not merely contrary but is devastating to reason. Let me show you why with help from another atheist, this time the bountifully bearded Daniel Dennett. His book *Consciousness Explained* was an attempt to show how science could answer perhaps the most difficult question of all: what is the human mind and how does it work. Here he is, in full swing:

> There is only one sort of *stuff*, namely matter – the physical stuff of physics, chemistry, and physiology – and the mind is somehow nothing but a physical phenomenon. In short, the mind is the brain ... we can (in principle!) account for every mental phenomenon using the same basic principles, laws, and raw materials that suffice to explain radioactivity, continental drift, photosynthesis, reproduction, nutrition, and growth.[174]

Did you grasp quite what Dennett said there? All that you are – your hopes and dreams, your beliefs and your values and, above all, your thinking and your reasoning – are nothing more than the movement of atoms jostling together, chemicals fizzing, neurons buzzing. Physics can explain your beliefs with the same ease that it can explain earthquakes or plant growth. But,

Penguin Books, 1997 [1955–1966].
173 My wife complained that I came back from our honeymoon in the Lake District with about 400 photographs, only about three of which actually had us in them.
174 Daniel Dennett, *Consciousness Explained*, Boston, MA: Little, Brown, 1991, p. 33.

hang on a moment, isn't there a problem here? Well, several, but one of the biggest is that continental drift and photosynthesis are not rational. I have occasionally been known to indulge in the odd glass of wine on a summer evening, but never, not even in my most, ahem, *relaxed* moments, have I ever thought to enquire of a newly grown leaf its view of politics or seek the advice of the Eurasian plate on the finer points of Shakespearian sonnets. So, if Dennett is right, something follows: those things are not rational, therefore *neither are we.* He's not alone in this idea. Here's another atheist, Colin Blakemore:

> The human brain is a machine which alone accounts for all our actions, our most private thoughts, our beliefs … All our actions are products of the activity of our brains. It seems to me to make no sense (in scientific terms) to try to distinguish sharply between acts that result from conscious attention and those that result from our reflexes or are caused by disease or damage to the brain.[175]

Again, that's the kind of paragraph you need to read twice to make sure that Colin really did say what you thought he said. Yes he did. Colin is claiming that it makes no sense – not just *little* sense, by the way, but *no* sense – to distinguish between acts that I carry out consciously and those that are caused by reflexes or even brain damage. Now I don't know about you, but I usually experience several reflexes in the course of a day. The occasional belch, the odd hiccough, several sneezes if the pollen count is running above average, nervous twitches when I read of the latest escapades of our political leaders. But never, not once, has it occurred to me that I ought to place the results

---

175 Colin Blakemore, *The Mind Machine*, London: BBC Books, 1990, p. 270.

of those reflexes on a par with my rational thoughts. Quite frankly, I really wish I'd thought of that before I spent ten years writing a PhD, as I could have got the thing completed far more quickly. I can envisage the viva in my mind's eye:

"Mr Bannister," my examiners would have asked, "we were managing to follow the argument you were developing in chapter two of your thesis, but then we came to pages fifty-six and fifty-seven, which were, how shall we put it – "

"A bit sticky?" I offer, helpfully.

"Well, yes." One of the examiners discreetly pulls out a bottle of hand sanitizer from her handbag.

"Ah, well that's a sneeze," I explain. "I thought it added somewhat to the argument. Similarly on pages one hundred and following, you'll find a spot where I had a spot of gas but thought I'd do something useful with it, so I recorded the footnotes on those pages as a series of belches."

Ridiculous as it may sound, I at least admire Dennett and Blackmore for trying to be consistent, even if the results are eye-wateringly bizarre. After all, if there is nothing that science cannot explain, then science must be able to explain everything, including your thought life. But how so? After all, given that the phenomena described by physics and chemistry are present in plate tectonics and photosynthesis, pebbles and amoebae, supernovae and sausages and silverfish and – well – everything, physics and chemistry are clearly not the places to be looking for answers to what it is that makes reason possible, unless, that is, you're really looking to explain reason away. As the late J. B. S. Haldane pointed out, if your thoughts are just a by-product of atoms jiggling in your brain, that may make them sound *chemically*, but it does not make them sound *logically*. And if that's the case then you've no reason to trust your initial belief that your mind is composed of atoms.[176] That's a circle that's not just vicious, but positively voracious and ravenous to boot.

Once you've explained away mind as a chemical reaction, thinking as a reflex, and selfhood as an illusion (a trick played on us by our genes, as one atheist put it to me), what precisely are you left with? When you've chopped, sliced, diced, and reduced the human mind you are left with nothing, and I emphasize *you* for a good reason – because, according to this description of reality, *you* don't exist. "You" are just a flickering of electrons, a fizzing of chemicals, a banging-together of atoms. The same can be said of continents as they drift, the firework as it explodes noisily, or the tea as it cools in the mug on your desk. Given that we're not going to grant personhood to them, what makes you so special? Why label this particularly temporary conglomeration of atoms and chemistry "Richard Dawkins" or "Daniel Dennett"? Why indeed. All of which begs a question: if human persons don't really exist, who precisely is it that is writing all these best-selling books of atheist literature? And, more to the point, who is banking the royalty cheques?[177] Perhaps my late grandmother's aphorism was true after all: empty vessels really do make the most noise. Or, as philosopher Mary Midgley put it more eloquently: "It is all very well to

---

176 J. B. S. Haldane, "When I Am Dead", in *On Being the Right Size and Other Essays*, Oxford: Oxford University Press, 1985, p. 30.

177 I remember once talking to a young doctoral student at Reading University who didn't believe that there was such a thing as the self. "I am just a succession of experiences," he announced boldly. "The so-called 'person' you're addressing now is not the 'person' you were speaking to even five minutes ago."

"Fascinating," I said. "By the way, when are you submitting your PhD thesis?"

"Early next year," he replied.

"Well done," I said. "Now, given what you've just said, the so-called 'person' who submits the thesis is not the series of so-called 'people' who wrote it. So do I take it you will immediately be reporting yourself to the university authorities for plagiarism?"

eliminate God from the intelligible universe but eliminating ourselves from it blocks all sorts of enquiries."[178]

❖

Maybe it's time to abandon the monomaniacal hammering of scientism. Don't get me wrong: I'm not anti-*science*; I love science, enjoying every moment that I studied it as a student (not least because science offered Bunsen burners and fire[179]). Science has answered many questions, has given us many technological advances, but nevertheless there are some questions it cannot answer and will never be able to answer. Now to admit that will provoke squeals of protest from some quarters, accusations that one is abandoning reason. But why should that be so? I'm simply arguing for "science *and*" – science *and* the humanities; science *and* philosophy; science *and* art; science *and* history; science *and* theology. Why must some atheists act like an agoraphobic toddler who is terrified of stepping outside the confines of the nursery into the garden, preferring to play with her building blocks and dollies inside where it's safe and familiar? Why can't we throw open the shutters, fling wide the doors, and embrace a world of knowledge that is vastly bigger and more glorious than just the physical sciences? Dawkins scoffs at such suggestions, muttering darkly of theology that "I [don't believe] in fairies at the bottom of the garden".[180] Well, guess what, Richard, neither

178 Mary Midgley, "Against Humanism", *New Humanist*, 25 October 2010 (http://rationalist.org.uk/2419/against-humanism).
179 My proudest scientific moment came aged thirteen, when I discovered in a physics class one afternoon that metal pencil sharpeners made in Germany contained a high proportion of magnesium. After I had idly heated one with a Bunsen burner for a couple of minutes, it suddenly exploded and lit up like a small sun. Rather than a Nobel Prize, I was rewarded with a detention, something that still irks to this day. But even Einstein had to start somewhere ...
180 Dawkins, *The God Delusion*, p. 74.

do I: but nor do I believe that we should napalm the flowerbeds, bulldoze the rockery, and concrete over the entire lawn in order to reduce things to a level you're more comfortable with.

Science, you see, has limits. Science comes to an end where, in fact, it opens up questions far bigger than itself. This is true, incidentally, whether, like me, you believe in God, or whether you don't. Consider, for example, the question of the origin of the universe. (A small question, nothing too taxing.) Scientists are divided on the answer to this. Some think the universe just popped into existence, uncaused, from nothing. Others believe that our universe is simply the latest in an infinite series of universes. Still others surmise that our universe is one of an endless collection of universes out there, the so-called multiverse, in which every reality plays itself.[181] Others, who have reflected deeply, believe that some kind of higher power, some kind of God created our universe. Now did you notice something about all four options: each one takes us *outside* science and does so for a very good reason. Science is a tool designed to deal with how the stuff of matter behaves. It is entirely the wrong tool – whether one is an atheist, an agnostic or a believer – to explain how we got stuff *in the first place*. A hammer is a marvellously handy thing for whacking in nails once you have them; it's a hopeless tool when it comes to explaining why nails exist in the first place.

One final thought. If there is an ultimate reality, if behind all that was and is and will be stands not the impersonal dancing of atoms or lifeless equations but a God of some kind, a God who is *personal*, that at least raises a number of possibilities. In particular, it goes a long way toward explaining why we too are

---

181 There is even one in which Richard Dawkins is a children's entertainer performing cheap illusions at birthday parties, such as making fish disappear: I guess one would call that the cod illusion.

personal creatures, beings who can communicate and think and reason, in a way that pebbles, pendulums, and petunias cannot. It may suggest, too, why we are so wired to pursue knowledge and discover truth, both in and beyond the sciences. Why humans are eternally restless and so indefatigably inquisitive. And it raises a third possibility, too: if that God is truly personal, then perhaps he has done what personal creatures do all the time – namely *communicate*. In which case we need to ask the next question: is there more that can be discovered about God than simply what we can discern about him from his handiwork as revealed in the structure of the universe? Is it possible to learn about the artist himself, not just his works? You see, if you want to know what I am really like, you could buy and read my books.[182] You could wait until I'm away on vacation, then break into my home and rifle through my personal papers. You could stalk me on Facebook and see what type of photographs and updates I post. All of those might get you somewhere. But there's an even better way: you could ask those who know me, or get to know me personally yourself. But, before you try that, do me a small favour, and put down that hammer …

For Further Reading

John Lennox, *God's Undertaker: Has Science Buried God?* (Oxford: Lion, 2009)

Alvin Plantinga, *Where the Conflict Really Lies: Science, Religion, and Naturalism* (Oxford: Oxford University Press, 2011)

David Stove, *Darwinian Fairytales: Selfish Genes, Errors of Heredity and Other Fables of Evolution* (New York: Encounter Books, 2007)

Raymond Tallis, *Aping Mankind: Neuromania, Darwinitis and the Misrepresentation of Humanity* (Durham: Acumen, 2012)

---

182 This would also make my publishers very happy.

8

Humpty Dumpty and the Vegan

(or: Why We Really Do Need God to Be Good)

"Bon appétit!" said the waiter with a smile, as he deposited a large pizza and a huge bowl of salad on our table. I looked at the food with something less than enthusiasm.

"Is anything wrong?" my friend asked.

"Nothing a slice of salami wouldn't solve," I muttered darkly. "Vegan pizzerias ... whatever next?"

"I'm really grateful you were willing to have lunch here," Garth said. "You know that I've been doing the whole faux Buddhist thing since I met Sally, so vegan food it is for me now. She's pretty insistent."

I poked the pizza tentatively with a fork: I've always been suspicious of vegetarian food and feel far more comfortable with meals that were once running around healthily in the fresh air, rather than rotting in the dampness of the soil. I looked up from my culinary investigations to see Garth produce a small

Tupperware container from his holdall. He glanced furtively around the restaurant to ensure that nobody was watching, and then shook out the contents over his half of the lunch.

"Whaassssat?" I enquired through a mouthful of avocado and lentil pizza.

"Tuna," he whispered.

I paused, mid-chew, like a cow that has just been struck by an idea. "Tuna?"

"Sssshhhh!" Garth hissed, putting a finger to his lips. "Not every vegan takes the liberal approach that I do; you'll get us thrown out of here."

Given that there was a burger restaurant across the street, that didn't sound such an unattractive proposition, but I couldn't let this one go. "Liberal approach?" I asked.

"Well, I don't really know what all the fuss is about," said Garth. "I eat fish. Big deal. Fish doesn't count as meat, does it? It can't be if it lives in water."

"Let me get this straight. You claim to be a vegan, but you eat fish?"

"Yes. And calamari – I've a friend who owes me a favour or two and can get it on the cheap."

"*Squid pro quo*, you might say."

"Exactly. Oh and I also still eat prawns, crab, shellfish, lobster. That kind of thing."

"Strangest vegan I've ever met," I said, staring at the salad bowl. I was sure I had just seen something crawl under a lettuce leaf.

"Duck, too," Garth added.

"Duck?" I exclaimed. Under the lettuce leaf, something was definitely wriggling.

"Well, they live in water, don't they?"

"So do hippopotami!"

"Now you're just being silly." Garth helped himself to a serving of salad. I thought it best not to mention what I'd just seen, as it had possessed rather a lot of legs.

"So you're claiming to be a vegan – telling your girlfriend, your colleagues, and your family that you're a vegan, subjecting your mates to vegan restaurants – all the while chowing down on anything that moves."

"That's not fair," protested Garth. "I'm not eating *anything*, just seafood and one or two other things." He took a mouthful of lettuce and chewed, increasingly thoughtfully.

"Like ducks."

"Like ducks. Oh, and cows; they live *near* water. There's a whole herd by the Thames near Clifton Hampden who often graze while standing *in* the river. That's practically aquatic." Garth discreetly spat a mouthful of lettuce, along with half a centipede, into an empty wine glass.

"So what you're telling me", I said, "is that any animal that lives in, on, near or within line of sight of water, or on a houseboat, is basically fair game."

Garth nodded. He reached into his bag again and produced another container, which appeared to contain some slices of salami.

"Dare I ask?"

"Venison sausage," he whispered. "It was your talk of 'fair game' that made me remember it."

I shook my head in despair. "Why not just come clean and admit that you're an omnivore like the rest of us? It's the hypocrisy that galls me, if I'm honest."

"*Hypocrisy*?" Garth spluttered, looking genuinely offended. "That's a bit strong, old chap. Quite frankly I would have expected somebody as well travelled as you to be a bit more, well, progressive."

"Progressive?"

"Yes. Besides, who says that *you* get to define what the word 'vegan' means, anyway? Who died and pronounced you king of the dictionary? I *say* 'vegan' to me means 'occasionally eats meat when there's a vowel in the month'. Tell me I'm wrong." Garth stared fiercely at me, daring me to disagree.

I wondered where to start: I wanted to take a stand for truth, for honesty, for consistency and coherence – but then there was the small matter of that rather insipid pizza. Sometimes you have to take the pragmatic route. "Pass me a few slices of that salami and I'll say no more about it."

⌘

The idea that words can mean whatever somebody wants them to mean is widespread in our culture, especially among the so-called New Atheist writers. The tendency is particularly evident when it comes to any words that have to do with morality – and gosh, do the New Atheists like to talk about morality. For all of their diversity, there is very much a common moral theme running through the recent crop of popular atheist books, especially concerning the question of good and evil. Men such as Richard Dawkins, Sam Harris, and others like them live in a very black and white, moral universe: violence, aggression, intolerance, ignorance, and, of course, religion and superstition are *bad*.[183] Conversely, humanism, generosity, kindness, and (it goes without saying) science, technology, and progress are *good*. And above all the moralizing, the stridency of which would impress a Victorian pamphleteer, ringing out loud and

---

183 No mention of goat's cheese, alas.

clear is the bigger claim: atheists do not need God in order to be good. Listen to these words from Alom Shaha, author of the *Young Atheist's Handbook*:

> Despite not believing in God, and not believing in an afterlife where I might be rewarded or punished for my behaviour, I try to be a good person. That's the most any of us can do.[184]

I may be an atheist, Alom is saying, but I can still be a decent, moral citizen. After all, isn't that what *all* of us are trying to be? Aren't we all basically good? That said, Alom isn't quite content to leave things there, but weaves into his statement hints of a further idea: that atheists are, in fact, *better* than religious people, because atheists do good for no ulterior motive. You religious types, the accusation goes, behave decently only because you believe that God is continually watching you, like a celestial headmaster with a CCTV camera in every room. But if God were to turn his back, even for an instant, if he were to take a week's holiday in the celestial equivalent of Benidorm, then you'd instantly launch into an explosion of wild living: riotous orgies, drinking to excess, shoplifting packets of Jammie Dodgers, poking small mammals with sticks, and generally being beastly. By contrast, atheists do good even when *nobody* is watching.[185]

The problem here is that the issue of goodness, God, and atheism is rather like two kittens and a ball of string, in that it gets pretty tangled very quickly, largely because people have a

---

184 Shaha, *The Young Atheist's Handbook*, p. 45.
185 I once saw the slogan "Atheists Do Good When Nobody Is Watching" on a bumper sticker. I had to fight the urge to tap on the car window and ask whether broadcasting the fact to all and sundry actually defeats the point, rather like my two-year-old daughter, who cries out "I'm hiding!" while crouching behind the sofa.

tendency to ask the wrong question. The question is not "Can somebody be good without God?" but rather, "What do we actually mean by the word 'good' in the first place?" As a child, I was a voracious reader, and among the books I loved were Lewis Carroll's stories of Alice's adventures in Wonderland. In the second of Carroll's two novels, *Through the Looking Glass*, Alice comes across the character of Humpty Dumpty, perched precariously high on a wall. They have a long conversation, in the course of which it quickly becomes apparent that Humpty Dumpty has the same eccentric approach to words as my friend Garth.

"I don't know what you mean by 'glory'," Alice said.

Humpty Dumpty smiled contemptuously. "Of course you don't – till I tell you. I meant 'there's a nice knock-down argument for you'!"

"But 'glory' doesn't mean 'a nice knock-down argument'," Alice objected.

"When *I* use a word," Humpty Dumpty said, in a rather scornful tone, "it means just what I choose it to mean – neither more nor less."

"The question is," said Alice, "whether you *can* make words mean so many different things."

"The question is," said Humpty Dumpty, "which is to be master – that's all."

Alice was much too puzzled to say anything; so after a minute Humpty Dumpty began again. "They've a temper, some of them – particularly verbs: they're the proudest – adjectives you can do anything with, but not verbs – however, *I* can manage the whole lot of them! Impenetrability! That's what *I* say."

"Would you tell me, please," said Alice, "what that means?"

"Now you talk like a reasonable child," said Humpty

Dumpty, looking very much pleased. "I meant by 'impenetrability' that we've had enough of that subject, and it would be just as well if you'd mention what you mean to do next, as I suppose you don't mean to stop here the rest of your life."

"That's a great deal to make one word mean," Alice said in a thoughtful tone.

"When I make a word do a lot of work like that," said Humpty Dumpty, "I always pay it extra."[186]

That little exchange, like my lunchtime discussion with my friend about his redefinition of the word "vegan", gets to the heart of this question about goodness. Simply put: who gets to define what the words "good" and "evil" mean? If we're not going to derive our understanding of goodness from the character and nature of God, for example, then from where? *Who*, precisely, gets to step into God's empty shoes and define the content of the word "good"? Now that's a crucial question, for unless we know what we mean by the word, then to proclaim that something is "good" is utterly meaningless. Just as if you saw a sign outside a high-street restaurant declaring "Special offer! Delicious vegetarian pizza just £1 per flopalob", you'd want to ask what a "flopalob" was,[187] so when somebody declares something "good" we can rightly ask what they mean by that word.

⌘

So how might we define the word "good" *sans* God? One option could be to engage in a bout of linguistic generosity and

---

186 Lewis Carroll, *Through the Looking Glass*, New York: Dover Publications, 1999, pp. 57–58.
187 As well as enquire what the word "delicious" was doing there next to the word "vegetarian".

allow everybody to define the word for themselves. Reckless though that may sound (I'm not sure I'd fly on an aircraft whose pilot believed he could define terms such as "airspeed" for himself), that is the way, practically speaking, that Western culture encourages us to behave. Tom decides that Marxism, vegetarianism, heterosexual serial monogamy, and animal liberation are the values he'll live by, and that's fine; those are good *for him*. But Bill, on the other hand, prefers hunting, gay marriage, and libertarianism. And, well, that's OK *too*. Those values, those pursuits, are likewise good *for him*. Provided that Tom and Bill can agree not to try to suggest that the other one is wrong, everybody can get along famously.

Maybe that seems like a flippant example, so let's go with a real one. A few decades back, Bertrand Russell, arguably the most famous atheist of the twentieth century, debated the Catholic philosopher Frederick Copleston. The discussion ranged across many topics but the subject of morality came up and Copleston put this question to Russell: "Dr Russell, tell me, as an atheist, how do you tell the difference between good and evil?"

"The same way I tell the difference between blue and yellow," Russell replied.

"But you distinguish between blue and yellow on the basis of *seeing*," said Copleston. "How do you tell the difference between good and evil?"

Russell thought for a moment before announcing: "On the basis of feeling."[188]

A moment's reflection on Russell's admission reveals a couple of things. First, he was probably right in that I suspect that it is on the basis of *feeling* that most people make their

188 A transcript of the debate can be found at http://www.scandalon.co.uk/ philosophy/cosmological_radio.htm. I have paraphrased for purposes of brevity and clarity.

moral choices. If it *feels* good, do it; if it *feels* bad (and I can't get away with it), don't. The problem is, of course, that we have feelings all the time. I feel hungry, I feel compassion; I feel cold, I feel cruel; I feel warm-hearted, I feel the gnawing pit of existential despair when watching England play international soccer. The question is, why go to the effort of labelling some of our feelings "good"? Why call my desire to help the old lady who lives next door across the street "good", my desire to lob a half-brick at Justin Bieber "evil", and my desire for a Jammie Dodger or an hour's nap ... well, just feelings? All feelings are equal, it would seem, but some feelings are more equal than others. The second problem is related: what happens when my feelings and your feelings clash? I feel we should save the poor little baby seals.[189] You feel we should club as many of the furry little vermin over the head as possible and make bedcovers out of their pelts. Who wins? Me, you, or the seal pups? Quite frankly, my first reaction, when I meet anybody who tells me that they sincerely believe that we decide what is "good" and "evil" based on our preferences or our feelings is to lean over and steal something from them. When they protest ("Give me back my seal-skin gloves!"), I simply say, innocently and sweetly: "But I thought you said 'good' and 'evil' were just questions of personal preference. Well, my preference is that I'm smitten with your mittens." That usually changes the conversation quite rapidly. Whatever Humpty Dumpty might say, words cannot simply mean whatever we want them to mean, no matter how much we pay them.

So if individuals can't be allowed carte blanche to define words for themselves, perhaps the answer is to swing to the other extreme and allow the state to decide what is good and

---

189 Not least because Brigitte Bardot says we should, and she used to be cute.

what is evil. That suggestion, I find, tends to get a slightly less than enthusiastic initial response. For sure, if we have a well-oiled system of representative democracy then we can simply elect our most trustworthy (or least untrustworthy, depending on your degree of cynicism) citizens into power and then the values they enshrine in law will have our blessing. Of course, it's potentially problematic if you're one of the 49 per cent who didn't vote for the ruling party and you disagree fundamentally with some law that is passed: does that mean you can simply ignore it? If not, then I guess we're saying that might makes right – that the will of the majority must triumph. That may be OK if the majority are busying themselves with parking policy or reforming the import tariffs on fish fingers and custard, but what if they start limiting the rights of minorities? What if the state in question is not a democracy at all, but one of those totalitarian nightmares whose leader's mental capabilities are not merely slightly ajar but positively unhinged? Again, we have to ask: does might make right?

In his book *The God Delusion*, Richard Dawkins has a lengthy section extolling what he calls the "The Changing Moral Zeitgeist", the way that he believes the world (by which he means those parts of it that bear a resemblance to North Oxford) is changing for the better, year after year, as societies enact more and more progressive legislation. Here he is in full flow:

> Some of us lag behind the advancing wave of the changing moral *Zeitgeist* and some of us are slightly ahead. But most of us in the twenty-first century are bunched together and way ahead of our counterparts in the Middle Ages, or in the time of Abraham, or even as recently as the 1920s.[190] The whole wave keeps moving

---

190 I had that reaction to *Downton Abbey*, too.

> ... Of course, the advance is not a smooth incline, but a meandering sawtooth ... But over the longer timescale, the progressive trend is unmistakable and it will continue.[191]

All of that poses a question. Well, not so much poses a question as erects it in forty-foot-high letters on the nearest mountain, paints them pink, and floodlights them for effect. Where are we progressing *to*? Progress implies a direction, doesn't it? If my wife phones me when I'm walking in the hills and asks: "How's the hike going?" and I reply: "I'm progressing", she'll assume that I am *nearer* my destination, rather than lost in the wilderness with one boot missing and my sandwiches stolen by a gang of marauding squirrels. So then, to *where* is society morally progressing: what's the destination? How will we know when we've arrived: will there be a sign and a teashop? If not, then what's the Magical Moral Standard enabling us to look at our culture today and say this is *better* than it was back *then*, if society *itself* determines what "good" means?

Consider a thought experiment. Let's imagine we were to mug a passing Time Lord and steal his time machine. We pull a few levers and zip back a few decades – just a short trip: the 1950s will do. Out we hop and find the nearest upright and upstanding member of the public. Twirling our bow tie,[192] we tell them that we're from the twenty-first century and explain what life is like there, during which we happen to mention that entirely non-controversial topic, gay marriage. Our new friend's jaw drops and they refuse to believe that such a thing exists – after all, how could something that their culture considers illegal, immoral, and entirely unacceptable in polite society flip to being legal,

---

191 Dawkins, *The God Delusion*, p. 303.
192 Bow ties are cool. (Geeks will spot the reference.)

promoted, and even encouraged just a few decades later? "How terribly unprogressive; thank goodness for Richard Dawkins and the Moral Zeitgeist!" we exclaim, clambering aboard our stolen TARDIS again and zipping back through the time vortex to the twenty-first century, arriving just *before* we stole it, thereby avoiding arrest but creating a temporal paradox at the same time. But then the thought hits us like a half-brick lobbed at a Justin Bieber concert: if it happened to *them*, it can happen to *us*. Anything that I, you, or society currently holds dear – our most treasured moral standards, our deepest values, those causes and judgments we consider absolutely unimpeachable – all could be overturned in a mere few decades. After all, we have the test case of gay marriage to prove it. So you can't call anything "good" on the basis of what society thinks, because society will very likely change its mind radically. The Moral Zeitgeist, it turns out, is not so much a sawtooth as a crazily scribbled line, drawn in crayon by a toddler on a sugar rush. It seems that we're no better off leaving society to determine what "good" and "evil" look like than we are allowing individuals to do so.

What we might call "Humpty Dumpty's Dilemma" – the question of *who* gets to decide what "good" means – was neatly illustrated in a famous paper written by the Yale University law professor Arthur Leff.[193] He points out that any moral claims (e.g. "You *ought* to help old ladies across the road"; "You *ought not* to poke badgers with a stick"; "Generosity *is* good"; "Paris Hilton *is* bad") – are *authority* claims, and to any authority claim we can respond like the school bully or the town drunk and cry: "Yeah? Sez *who*?" In the absence of God, says Leff, there are but two options: you can turn every individual person into a little godlet, able to decide good and evil for themselves. But then

193 Arthur A. Leff, "Unspeakable Ethics, Unnatural Law", *Duke Law Journal* 6, 1979, pp. 1229–1249. Available online at http://bit.ly/leff.

who evaluates between them when there are clashes between godlet claims? Alternatively, you can turn the state into God and let it determine good and evil, but then might becomes right and you have sheer, naked brutality (and what's wrong with government-sponsored brutality, if the state *is* the only moral authority?) In short, if you try this latter route, morality becomes *meaningless*. If you go down the former route, morality becomes *impossible*. And in either case, whenever another godlet, or the state, tells you that anything is good, right, or the Proper Thing To Do, you can look them squarely in the eye and sneer: "Really, sez *who*?" Leff ends his essay by pointing out that there is only one solution to this – and that would be if goodness were something *bigger* than us, something outside us. Only then could ethics, morality, and law actually work:

> Only if ethics were something unspeakable by us, could law be unnatural, and therefore unchallengeable. As things now stand, everything is up for grabs.
> Nevertheless:
> Napalming babies is bad.
> Starving the poor is wicked.
> Buying and selling each other is depraved.
> Those who stood up to and died resisting Hitler, Stalin, Amin, and Pol Pot – and General Custer too – have earned salvation.
> Those who acquiesced deserve to be damned.
> There is in the world such a thing as evil.
> [All together now:] Sez who?
> God help us.[194]

⌘

---

194   Ibid., p. 1249.

"Hang on just a minute!" I can hear some cry at this point. "Surely there are *plenty* of ways we can determine good and evil, morality, and ethics without God. We can use science!" That's the approach taken by Sam Harris, whose book *The Moral Landscape: How Science Can Determine Human Values* attempts to do exactly what it says on the tin. I do give Harris credit for at least realizing something that many other atheist writers have failed to grasp – that atheism has a major problem when it comes to the question of goodness. But Harris thinks he has the solution. No need for philosophy or theology or any other dusty ology for *him*; he can square the circle using *science*. How so? Well, the key, says Harris, is carefully defining what we mean by "morality":

> [Q]uestions about values – about meaning, morality, and life's larger purpose – are really questions about the well-being of conscious creatures. Values, therefore, translate into facts that can be scientifically understood. ... If there are objective truths to be known about human well-being – if kindness, for instance, is generally more conducive to happiness than cruelty is – then science should one day be able to make very precise claims about which of our behaviors and uses of attention are morally good, which are neutral, and which are worth abandoning.[195]

In other words, questions about morality are really questions about human flourishing and specifically about *happiness*. What is *good* is really a question of what makes the greatest number of people happy, and science can help with that (ensuring that we're healthy, for instance), and thus science can answer questions of morality.

195 Sam Harris, *The Moral Landscape: How Science Can Determine Human Values*, New York: Free Press, 2011, pp. 1–2, 8.

When I was thirteen years old, one of my hobbies was conjuring. Every Saturday morning I faithfully trekked across London to attend conjuring classes at Davenports Magic Shop, an Aladdin's cave of a store which was all the more wondrous for being located in an underground mall deep beneath Charing Cross. I was drawn to the practice of prestidigitation by many things: the fun of fooling people, the sense of superiority afforded by the ability to outwit the school bully at the three-card trick, and also a beautiful fellow student named Paula.[196] Those classes taught me to recognize a good trick when I see one, and Harris's paragraph above is a fine trick. It's one thing to pull a rabbit from a hat, but Harris produces a hippopotamus, two penguins, and a family of meerkats. And, like any good trick, we want to ask how he did it. How, *precisely*, does "morality" become transformed into "well-being" and "happiness", at least without major helpings of pixie dust?

You see, there are a number of problems with trying to use science like this. First, why choose to maximize *happiness*? Why not choose knowledge? Or compassion? Or bravery? Or stamp-collecting?[197] In short, science cannot tell us *why* we should value happiness over and above all other virtues or pursuits. Indeed, if happiness is all that counts, why not simply hook us all up to machines wired directly to the pleasure centres of our brains and we can see out our days in happy delirium. Most of us instinctively sense the problem there: indeed, to paraphrase the philosopher John Stuart Mill: "Better to be an unhappy Socrates than a very happy pig." But if we *must* stick with happiness, well here's another question for Harris: why is

---

196 Readers who recall the reasons I shared in chapter two for learning the cello may spot a pattern. Whenever a teenage boy takes up a new hobby, you can bet that somewhere there's a girl he's trying to impress.

197 Philately will get you everywhere.

your happiness worth the same as *my* happiness? From where are you deriving the Magical Moral Standard that meticulously evens out the playing field with spirit-level precision and allows us to conclude that everybody has an equal right to be happy? After all, it's perfectly possible that somebody else's happiness is best served at your expense. For instance, let's imagine that I have three friends: a professor of medicine who is about to find the cure for both the common cold and Justin Bieber; a philanthropist who is on the verge of giving billions of dollars to Greenpeace and the Harlech Male Voice Choir[198]; and a world-famous politician who is about to solve the Middle East crisis. But there's a problem: the professor has a failing heart; the philanthropist has two distinctly dodgy kidneys; and the politician's liver is waving a white flag. But wait! By happy coincidence, you, dear reader, turn out to be an unemployed, homeless layabout, with no friends or family. So all we need do is euthanize you (painlessly, of course – what *do* you take us scientists for?) and then we can cannibalize you for spare parts to save the other three. Just think of the net gain in happiness that would produce.

You see, despite Harris's enthusiastic suggestion that science can solve questions of goodness and morality, we're still sunk to the top of our gumboots in the middle of Humpy Dumpty's Dilemma – what is it that gives Harris, or indeed any scientist, the right to start telling *us* what "morality" means? For all of their being dressed up in a white laboratory coat and paraded under clean fluorescent lighting, claims that science can give us goodness without God are just a sophisticated version of the "might makes right" thesis, to which we can respond (altogether now): "Sez *who*?"

---

198 Thereby saving both the whales and the wails of Wales.

If science cannot provide the grounds for morality, there's one last option that is sometimes trotted out by New Atheists keen to clobber God over the head but to hang on to some semblance of ethics: evolution. For those who appeal to so-called "evolutionary ethics", the solution to our quandary is to see morality as a biological adaptation. In the evolutionary story, every organism is engaged in a struggle to survive and those features that better enable a critter to thrive and reproduce will be selected for – whether that's the giraffe's long neck, the dog's ability to hear a refrigerator door open from 100 yards away, or the human sense of morality. Here's atheist Michael Ruse explaining how he thinks this might work:

> Darwin himself recognized that although the struggle for existence can lead to open conflict, it does not necessarily do so. Often one can get more out of life by cooperating rather than by fighting. This is fairly obvious when we think about it. Suppose there is some desirable resource, let us say a freshly killed animal that is a major source of protein. Two rivals might do much better by deciding to share the booty rather than fighting over it.[199]

Now perhaps Ruse is onto something: after all, fourteen years of married life has taught me the lesson that sharing the Cadbury's Dairy Milk chocolate, rather than scoffing the lot and then engaging in sticky-fingered denials, leads to much more harmonious evenings in the Bannister household. But can appeals to evolution go the whole way and actually get us to a godless morality? No, not really. The first problem is that what Ruse describes is not actually morality at all, but merely

199 Michael Ruse, "Naturalist Moral Nonrealism", in R. Keith Loftin (ed.), *God & Morality: Four Views*, Downers Grove, IL: IVP, 2012, pp. 53–74, citing p. 58.

a description of behaviour.[200] Natural selection has chosen the lion's pointy teeth, the seagull's streamlined wings, and the baboon's bright red bottom – but not because they are right, or good, or proper; simply because they get the job done (fighting, fleeing, feeding, or reproducing). So, if the reason that human beings are inclined to cooperate is that natural selection worked out that this was a good survival strategy, that doesn't make it *good* – it just makes it *work*. Calling things like sharing, cooperation, and altruism "moral" or "good" is like my calling a tin opener "moral" or a mousetrap "good". They are no such thing; they are purely functional.

Next up is the problem that appealing to evolution to explain morality rather sloppily confuses "innate" with "authoritative". Just because I find an urge within myself, how precisely – by what *criterion* – do I decide whether it is "good" and whether or not I should obey it? Evolution may have equipped me with the desire to help old ladies across the road and to give generously to the poor. But it's also equipped me with the desire to eat too much chocolate, tell poor jokes at inappropriate occasions, and lob half-bricks at trendily coiffured musical miscreants. Which of those urges should I obey? Some of them? *All* of them? How do I decide? Evolutionary morality leads to some very curious quirks, too, such as the bizarre conclusion that we cannot criticize the past. You see, if morality *evolves* (think back to Dawkins and his Moral Zeitgeist), then presumably we, sophisticated and clean-living denizens of the twenty-first century, are more moral, more *evolved*, than our forefathers. And so, when we look back and see our eighteenth-century ancestors engaging in such atrocities as the slave trade, what

---

200 See the wonderfully witty David Stove, *Darwinian Fairytales: Selfish Genes, Errors of Heredity and Other Fables of Evolution*, New York: Encounter Books, 2007, especially pp. 115–171.

we must conclude is that they simply hadn't evolved far enough to know that this was wrong.[201] But of course, if that's the case, denouncing them for enslaving millions of men, women, and children is on a par with my criticizing my cat for not yet having evolved thumbs and thus being unable to open the cat-food tin unaided. "Should have done better?" queries the cat, pausing as it licks its bum,[202] "Sez who, mate?"

⌘

Despite the myriad difficulties that beset attempts to ground goodness without God, morality is *everywhere*. We simply can't help ourselves – we open our mouths and moral judgments tumble out. The person who cut us up in traffic on the way to work is *bad*; fairly traded chocolate is *good*; Nelson Mandela and Martin Luther King were *moral*; those who cheat at cricket are *immoral*. I got that last example from Richard Dawkins, by the way. Back in the summer of 2013, at the height of the Ashes Test Series against Australia, English cricketer Stuart Broad allegedly engaged in some unsportsmanlike behaviour by not admitting that the ball had nicked the edge of his bat before it was caught. While a cricket match may move, at least to North American eyes, with slow glacial majesty, it is a game high on chivalry, and Broad's actions caused huge controversy. It turns out that Richard Dawkins is a cricket fan and so he took to Twitter to protest:

---

201 Furthermore, if it is society that determines what is "good", then to question or to resist society must thus make you, by definition, "evil". In which case, someone like William Wilberforce, the famous anti-slavery campaigner, must actually have been a moral reprobate and his commemorative statue in Westminster Abbey should be ground up forthwith. The resultant gravel could be used to pave the highway for the Moral Zeitgeist Express as it whizzes along.

202 I'm convinced that cats do this to take away the taste of the cat food.

> Stuart Broad obviously knew perfectly well he was caught. Refused to walk. What a revolting cheat. I now want Australia to win the Ashes.[203]

He followed this up with:

> I am well aware that it is a fact that professional cricketers care about winning more than about morality. But they bloody well shouldn't.[204]

When I first read this flurry of tweets,[205] I must confess that I found them exceedingly curious. This, after all, is the *same* Richard Dawkins who has argued that, when it comes to explaining all of life, evolution is the "only game in town". Indeed, in his book *River Out of Eden*, Dawkins penned this oft-quoted passage:

> The universe we observe has precisely the properties we should expect if there is, at bottom, no design, no purpose, no evil and no good, nothing but blind, pitiless indifference. As that unhappy poet A. E. Housman put it:
>
> > "For Nature, heartless, witless Nature
> > Will neither know nor care."
>
> DNA neither knows nor cares. DNA just is. And we dance to its music.[206]

---

203 Richard Dawkins (@RichardDawkins), 12 July 2013, 5:38 p.m., https://twitter.com/RichardDawkins/status/355803363834732544.

204 Richard Dawkins (@RichardDawkins), 12 July 2013, 6:11 p.m., https://twitter.com/RichardDawkins/status/355811671723347969.

205 I'm grateful to Phill Sacre, "Richard Dawkins on the Ethics of Stuart Broad", http://phillsacre.me.uk/2013/07/15/richard-dawkins-on-the-ethics-of-stuart-broad for first putting me on to this.

206 Richard Dawkins, *River Out of Eden: A Darwinian View of Life*, New York: Basic Books, 1995, p. 133.

But if nature really is neither good nor evil, if we are all simply dancing to our DNA, gyrating to our genes, then from which top hat has Dawkins produced this moral standard with which he's whacking hapless cricketers over the head? There's only one way you can make the value judgment that Dawkins brandishes here, and that's if life has some kind of *purpose*, a way that you, I, and Stuart Broad are *supposed to live*. The difference between a game of cricket and the game of life – in an atheistic universe anyway– is that cricket has rules but life does not; at least not any purpose beyond reproducing our DNA, if Dawkins is correct.

I'm grateful that Dawkins raises the question of purpose, because I believe it is the key to unlocking this whole question of good and evil. Have you ever noticed that it is "purpose" that enables us to determine whether something is being used rightly? For instance, should you catch me attempting to use my lawnmower to clean the leaves from my swimming pool,[207] a cricket bat to whisk eggs, or tightly rolled-up pages I have ripped from the paperback edition of *The God Delusion* as supporting struts in a rival to the Forth Road Bridge that I am constructing at North Queensferry, I imagine you would rebuke me with the words "That's not their intended *purpose*". And you'd be quite right too. But if we inherently recognize purpose when it comes to cricket bats, lawnmowers, and books, what about *life*? Does human life have a purpose: is there something that I, you, and human society are *supposed* to be? To ask this is to raise the question of what the ancient Greek philosophers called *telos* – the purpose, end, or goal of life. If there is such a thing, then that which aligns or orientates with it is *good* and that which does not is *evil*. As the Harvard political philosopher Michael

---

207 It's actually just a £20 inflatable paddling pool from a catalogue store, but everybody is entitled to a delusion of grandeur now and again.

Sandel puts it in his book *Justice: What's the Right Thing to Do*:

> Debates about justice and rights are often, unavoidably, debates about the purpose of social institutions, the goods they allocate, and the virtues they honour and reward. Despite our best efforts to make law neutral on such questions, it may not be possible to say what's just without arguing about the nature of the good life.[208]

Unless you're willing to tackle the question of the "good life", the question of *telos*, of purpose, then you cannot actually address questions of morality, for you have no way of knowing what a human life is supposed to be. Maybe the lawnmower *can* clear the leaves from the pool, if I just duct-tape enough water wings onto it and manage to avoid getting electrocuted in the process; maybe a cricket bat *can* whisk eggs, if I move it really fast and the eggs are really big; maybe my paper-based engineering project *can* work, if the cars are really tiny and the winds are not blowing too hard; maybe I can engage in tax evasion, serial philandering, slavery, or genocide, if my life is mine to make of it what I will, and damn the consequences: "I'm wrong, you claim? Sez *who*?"

There's only one solution to all of this, and that is if there is a source of goodness that is bigger than and above and beyond us – a *transcendent* source of goodness, perhaps what the Greek philosopher Plato called "The Good" (capital T, capital G), from which all morals and values, opinions and choices, decisions and actions ultimately derive their value. Perhaps that source of all goodness might also provide something more: perhaps it might help with the question of purpose, giving us a

---

208 Michael J. Sandel, *Justice: What's the Right Thing to Do?*, New York: Farrar, Straus and Giroux, 2010, p. 207.

clue that we are not mere cosmic accidents, churned up from the genetic cauldron of chaos, but instead that we were made *for* something, fashioned to *be* something; maybe, too, says Christianity, intended to *know* someone. Of course, if there is such a transcendent source of goodness, it raises some troubling issues quite quickly, one of which being what the implications are if we fall short of it. After all, if goodness is not something controlled by us, not just a word hammered into shape on an anvil of our own making, then, heaven forbid, it might turn out that we're *not* actually good. If "good" is under my control, there's a natural tendency to assume that I'm it, and *those* people over there are *bad*. But if the darned thing is transcendent – well, it might turn out that I'm as messed-up as the rest of the human race. After all, isn't the whole point of a standard that it enables us to see what or who does not measure up? What if the answer, at one level, is "none of us"?

The uncomfortable questions that all of this stirs up are one reason, I suspect, why many atheists find it's much safer to erect "Road Closed" signs and barricade the intersection. This is rapidly becoming not just a philosophical discussion but a highly personal one. Besides, talk of transcendent sources of goodness, of The Good, even, sound dangerously close to "God talk" – and haven't we slammed the front door firmly in *his* face? The last thing we need him doing is hopping over the back wall, sauntering up the lawn and in through the patio windows. To which I say: fine, write God's obituary, announce that transcendent sources of goodness are a philosopher's pipe dream, and declare that we are alone in an atheistic universe. But, if you do that, realize that any talk of "good" and "evil" is at once rendered entirely meaningless. Indeed, to declare "I can be good without God" is akin to claiming "I can be a vegan and eat meat" or "I can be celibate while sleeping my way through the women's hockey team", or perhaps, more poignantly, "I can enjoy the morning sunshine on the deck, even while adamantly denying that the sun actually exists". Without a transcendent source of goodness, then quite frankly Humpty Dumpty was right: the word "good" can mean *anything at all*. So, for sure, an atheist can be "good", but so can a garden gnome, a packet of goat's cheese, or a rubber chicken. "A *good* atheist, you say? Sez *who*?"

For Further Reading

Paul Chamberlain, *Can We Be Good Without God? A Conversation About Truth, Morality, Culture & a Few Other Things That Matter* (Downers Grove, IL: IVP, 1996)

C. S. Lewis, *The Abolition of Man* (New York: HarperOne, 2001 [1944])

R. Keith Loftin (editor), *God & Morality: Four Views* (Downers Grove, IL: IVP, 2012)

Michael J. Perry, *Toward a Theory of Human Rights: Religion, Law, Courts* (New York: Cambridge University Press, 2007)

Michael J. Sandel, *Justice: What's the Right Thing to Do?* (New York: Farrar, Straus and Giroux, 2010)

9

The Peculiar Case of the Postmodern Penguin

(or: Why Life Without God is Meaningless)

Last night I had the strangest of dreams. Perhaps it was a combination of too large a helping of cheese, the wildlife documentary I'd watched before retiring, and the flurry of snowflakes whirling outside my window;[209] whatever the precise causes, my dream took me to the frozen tundra of the South Pole. The sky was azure blue overhead, the sun sparkled on the ice, and all was quiet and still. Only the occasional cry of a seabird or the mating call of a wandering environmentalist broke the silence.

I walked for miles, my feet scrunching in the fresh snow; I passed great glaciers, cliffs of ice, and mountains of jagged rock. Finally I crested a small ridge and there before me was the most marvellous sight: in the valley below me, stretched out as far as the eye could see, was an enormous penguin colony. Thousands of black and white birds were huddled together, shuffling their

---

209 It was summer in Toronto.

feet to keep warm, each standing on its own square metre of ice. Entranced, I strolled slowly forward, remembering what David Attenborough had said about penguins being fairly tame.[210] Aside from the odd *aark!* of protest and the occasional peck at my knees, the birds tolerated my presence. In due course, my walking brought me to the edge of the ice floe on which the penguin colony lay, and as I stood at the water's edge, surrounded by the vast throng of birds, looking out across the waves of the Southern Ocean, I reflected on the fact that, beautiful as all this was, it must be a pretty bleak existence.

"I'm glad I'm not a penguin," I mused out loud. "What an entirely futile life this must be."

"How *dare* you!" squeaked a tiny voice, barely audible above the general cacophony of the colony.

I looked around, startled. Was I imagining things?

"Down *here*," came the voice again. I looked down to see a plump little penguin, identical to all of its fellows apart from the fact that this one was wearing a knitted tea cosy on its head.

"Did – did you just speak?" I asked, incredulously.

"I *did*," said the penguin, preening a wing. "It's a dream, you dummy; what were you expecting? Verisimilitude?"

I wondered quite what had been in that cheese. "Why are you wearing a tea cosy?" I asked.

"It's a hat."

"Looks like a tea cosy to me."

"If I *say* it's a hat, it's a hat," snapped back the penguin, stamping a little webbed foot. "Now, what was that you were muttering about a penguin's life being futile?"

"I'm sorry," I replied, "I didn't mean to be rude; it's just that, how shall I put this ...?"

---

210 Especially the milk-chocolate variety.

"Don't mince your words on *my* account; *I'm* just a penguin, apparently."

"Well, my point was simply that here you are, stuck on a lonely ice floe, with nothing to do other than huddle together for warmth in a multitude of identical birds with little more to look forward to than the next fish. Occasionally, I assume, you make baby penguins, who'll then repeat the whole meaningless cycle all over again. Sounds a *whole* lot of fun to me."

"Guano," said the penguin.

"Well, that's a bit strong."

"No, no, you're standing in the guano." The penguin pointed with a wing. I looked down to see that I was, indeed, standing in a puddle of penguin poop. The problem was that every other inch of ice for as far I could see was similarly covered.

The penguin gave a neighbour a shove. "Move up a bit, Frank; make some room." His neighbour squawked grumpily, and then dived into the ocean with a splash. "Well, I disagree with *everything* you've just said," said the penguin, snorting as derisively as it's possible to do with a beak. "My life is *full* of meaning."

"How so?"

"Because I've *created* meaning. Sure, I may be stuck here with all these other dumb birds, up to my unhappy feet in frozen bird poop in an often howling gale,[211] in darkness for six months of the year, but I've made my own meaning."

"You have?"

"Oh, yes. My life is *very* meaningful. I take frequent swims to that iceberg – " (the penguin gestured with a wing) – "and back. I hum little ditties. I dream up new sushi recipes. I compose limericks. I watch dolphins swim by."

---

211 Guano with the wind.

"Your life has porpoise, you mean?"

"Ha!" said the penguin, pecking my leg with its beak. "You're too small-minded, that's your problem. More imagination needed! Just because I'm stuck on an ice floe it doesn't prevent me from *inventing* a meaning for my life, thank you very much. I can transcend ice and guano, I can soar above the gnawing monotony of existence, I can waddle free of existential restraints, I can – "

What else my fat little friend could do, I'm afraid I can't tell you, because at that point the waters in front us ripped violently apart and the largest sea lion I have ever seen leapt from the deep, opened its massive maw and swallowed the penguin whole – feathers, philosophy, and all. Then, pausing only to wink at me, it plunged back beneath the icy waves. A tattered tea cosy floated sadly on the briny surf.

"Bummer when that happens," said a passing seagull.

I looked up in surprise. "You can talk *too*?"

"Lay off the Roquefort next time, that's my advice."

⌘

A recent poll for a major Internet search company ranked "What is the meaning of life?" as the toughest question of all, coming far above such other existential stumpers as "What is love?", "Do blondes have more fun?", and "Why do you never see baby pigeons?"[212] In his novel *The Hitchhiker's Guide to the Galaxy*, Douglas Adams imagines the building of a super computer, Deep Thought, designed to answer the question of life's meaning once and for all. Despite major protests from the Amalgamated Union of Philosophers, Sages, Luminaries and Other Thinking Persons ("I mean what's the use of our

---

212 I suspect because they're incredibly tiny when they first hatch and then they rapidly inflate, rather like avian popcorn.

sitting up half the night arguing that there may or may not be a God if this machine only goes and gives us his bleeding phone number the next morning?"[213]), the computer is switched on and allowed to ponder the question. After seven and a half million years of cogitation, Deep Thought is finally ready to announce the answer: the *final* answer, the *objective* answer, the *definitive* answer to the Great Question of Life, the Universe and Everything:

> "I don't think," said Deep Thought, "that you're going to like it."
>
> "Doesn't matter!" said Phouchg. "We must know it! Now!"
>
> "Now?" inquired Deep Thought.
>
> "Yes! Now ..."
>
> "Alright," said the computer and settled into silence again. The two men fidgeted. The tension was unbearable.
>
> "You're really not going to like it," observed Deep Thought.
>
> "Tell us!"
>
> "Alright," said Deep Thought. "The Answer to the Great Question ..."
>
> "Yes ...!"
>
> "Of Life, the Universe and Everything ..." said Deep Thought.
>
> "Yes ...!"
>
> "Is." said Deep Thought, and paused.
>
> "Yes ...!"
>
> "Is ..."
>
> "Yes ... !!! ...?"
>
> "Forty-two," said Deep Thought, with infinite majesty and calm.

---

213 Douglas Adams, *The Hitchhiker's Guide to the Galaxy*, New York: Harmony Books, 1979, p. 172.

> It was a long time before anyone spoke. Out of the corner of his eye Phouchg could see the sea of tense expectant faces down in the square outside.
>
> "We're going to get lynched, aren't we?" he whispered.[214]

When it is later suggested to Deep Thought that this answer is somewhat anticlimactic, the computer retorts that the problem is possibly that nobody knew what the question actually was with any precision.[215] This minor digression into science fiction serves to remind us that any answer to the question of life's meaning and purpose is not going to come easily, but is going to be hard won. Nevertheless, it is a vital question, because your answer to it is one that you will implicitly live by. What you think the meaning of life is will shape your values, ideals, beliefs, hopes, dreams, and opinions as well as the bumper stickers that you slap on the rear fender of your VW. And when life turns sour – whether it's the loss of a loved one, the end of a career, or when the markets crash and a graph of your stock portfolio's value looks like the black-diamond run at a ski resort frequented by nihilistic masochists – what you think the meaning to life is will shape how you deal with adversity. As Friedrich Nietzsche put it: "He who has a *why* to live for can bear with almost any *how*".[216]

Now Nietzsche, of course, was an atheist – it was he who famously popularized the sound bite "God is dead" – and so that raises an important question: is it actually *possible* for life to have meaning if God doesn't exist? If there is no God, if we are alone in an atheistic universe, the human race thrown up

---

214 Ibid., pp. 179–181.
215 Which sums up most of the problem with Google.
216 Cited in Viktor E. Frankl, *Man's Search for Meaning*, New York: Pocket Books, 1997, p. 126.

like flotsam and jetsam on the tides of time, chance, and chaos, then isn't life meaningless, valueless, and purposeless? And, if we attempt to protest to the contrary, are we not in exactly the same position as my feathery Antarctic friend? Well, protest to the contrary many atheists do; listen to these stirring words from Molleen Matsumura:

> We humanists agree that there is no karmic law, no Grand Plan, and no Grand Planner to make the world make sense for us. Instead of discovering "The Meaning of Life," we're faced with the job of *creating meaningful lives for ourselves*.[217]

Similarly fine words can be found falling from the lips and keyboards of many atheists and humanists; here's a second example, this time from the Humanist Canada website:

> Humanism is a philosophy or life-stance based upon a profound respect for human dignity and the conviction that human beings are ultimately accountable to themselves and to society for their actions. It is a deity-free worldview that affirms *our ability to lead ethical and meaningful lives without reliance upon a belief in the supernatural*.[218]

Both statements are powerful, emotive, and crystal clear: atheists don't need God, or deities, or heaven, or an afterlife, or the supernatural, or Joel Osteen, or indeed anything outside us – we can create meaning for ourselves. There may be no picture on the outside of the jigsaw box that is life, but don't let that stop us: we can by our own wit, charm, cleverness,

---

217 Molleen Matsumura, "Ingredients of a Life Worth Living", in Dale McGowan et al. (editors), *Raising Freethinkers: A Practical Guide for Parenting Beyond Belief*, New York: AMACOM, 2009, p. 129 (emphasis mine).

218 Source: http://humanistcanada.ca/about/humanism (emphasis mine).

and sheer Herculean effort create meaning for ourselves. Just as my twenty-two-month-old daughter has discovered that most jigsaw pieces will fit if you stamp on them hard enough (or chew the knobbly bits off), so we can do the same when it comes to life, the universe, and everything: I can (*thwack!*) find meaning (*thump!*) in life (*wallop!*) for myself (*clobber!*). If there were a soundtrack other than percussion accompanying all of this, it'd probably be Frank Sinatra's "My Way". Over the years, I have lost count of the times I have heard humanists and atheists recount versions of this narrative, often followed by a little stamp of the foot and an I-dare-you-to-disagree-with-me glint in their eye. But I am afraid that I must politely disagree: let me explain why.

The first problem with the idea that we can simply create our own meaning, whipping up a little purpose as though creating a novel variety of soufflé, is that it assumes that the universe cares. For the sake of argument, let us imagine that the universe is All That There Is. Think about that universe with awe and wonder for a moment: 13.8 billion years old, as ancient as time itself; over 92 billion light years wide; containing stars and supernovae, galaxies and gas clouds too numerous to count: a universe compared to which you are less than an infinitesimally microscopic speck of sand on a seashore that stretches from horizon to horizon. As atheist cosmologist Lawrence Krauss memorably expressed it: "We are a 1% bit of pollution within the universe. We are completely insignificant."[219] Before that

---

219 Cited in Amanda Lohrey, "The Big Nothing: Lawrence Krauss and Arse-Kicking Physics", *The Monthly*, October 2012 (http://www.themonthly.com.au/issue/2012/october/1354074365/amanda-lohrey/big-nothing). Here's a piece of fun, geeky mathematics: it is generally accepted that the known universe contains 1×10^{80} atoms. Meanwhile, an average human being contains 7×10^{27} atoms and there are approximately 7 billion humans alive today (7×10^9). Multiply those two together and we get the total number of atoms in all humans: roughly 4.9×10^{37}. That means that the percentage of all

universe the atheist purports to stand and say: "Well, I don't care *how* big you are, mate; I've created meaning for my life!" The poet Stephen Crane pricks the pomposity of this:

> A man said to the universe:
> "Sir, I exist!"
> "However," replied the universe.
> "The fact has not created in me
> A sense of obligation."[220]

Why should we imagine that the universe owes us something, that if we jump up and down and shout loudly enough the cosmos will stoop down and lend us an ear? If reality really does consist of nothing more than the slow, inexorable grind of the forces of physics, if you and I are governed by the same physical laws that drive quarks, quasars, and quails, then life doesn't suddenly acquire meaning just because *I* say it does. Indeed, as Richard Dawkins put it: "We should not think there's anything special about us. We used to think we were the centre of the universe[221] and now we know we're not."[222] For sure, there's nothing to stop you making as many eloquent pronouncements about the meaning of life as you wish, but it's only a matter of time before you fall foul of the next virulent virus, falling

---

atoms that are currently busying themselves forming part of a human being is 4.9×10^{-43}%. Krauss, however, claims we are a '1% bit of pollution' – making him off by a factor of 2×10^{40}. For non-mathematicians, that's a 2 with 40 zeros after it. Let's be grateful Krauss is a cosmologist, not an economist.

220 Stephen Crane, *War is Kind and Other Poems*, New York: Dover Publications, 1998, p. 36.

221 I currently live in Toronto, which like many major cities can sometimes lazily assume that it's the centre of the universe, much to the irritation of folks who live elsewhere in the country. When I hear that complaint raised, mollification can sometimes be facilitated by pointing out that things revolve around axes, for sure, but they also orbit around plug holes.

222 Cited in Russell Stannard, *Science and Wonders*, London: Faber and Faber, 1996, p. 72.

rock, toy car at the top of the stairs, passing sea lion, or any of the other multifarious ways that the universe reserves for the dispatching of squishy carbon-based life forms, leaving your voice as just an echo in the wind.

⌘

Cheerful stuff, eh? But chin up, for we're just getting started: there are many further problems with the idea that we can mould our own meaning. For instance, what happens if my meaning contradicts your meaning? Let's imagine that you decide that meaning to your life will be found by embracing the cause of environmentalism: you buy only locally sourced organic food; install solar panels on your roof; plant a tree for every puff of carbon dioxide that you guiltily emit; you even drive a clockwork Prius. You are, quite frankly, greener than a seasick landlubber canoeing her way round Cape Wrath in a hurricane. But I, on the other hand, decide that the meaning of *my* life will be to have a carbon footprint bigger than Sasquatch's. I have my morning coffee flown in each morning from Peru; I install a vast coal-fired turbine in the shed; I invest in strip-mining and clear-cutting operations in the Amazon; and, to cap it all, I drive a Hummer. You couldn't find two more different approaches to life if you locked Jeremy Clarkson and Al Gore in a broom cupboard. So who wins? My "meaning" and your "meaning" are so vastly, staggeringly, cataclysmically different that there's simply no reconciling them. And given we've already admitted that on atheism there's no meaning "baked" into reality, no "right answer", as it were, then I guess we're left to fight it out. (Although I'll take my petrol-powered lightsaber over your solar-powered potato peeler anytime, especially if it's a cloudy day.)

To appreciate the kind of pickle we're in, if "meaning" is simply something everybody gets to make up for themselves, think about another context in which we use the word. Consider literature for a moment: indeed, contemplate that wildly popular atheist manifesto, *The God Delusion*. What's Richard Dawkins's book actually about; what's its *meaning*? Well, suppose I were to read it and conclude that it's really a cookery book. Based on the meaning that I believe I have found in the book, I proceed to create a culinary cornucopia of cakes, trifles, and puddings. You, on the other hand, well you read *The God Delusion* and decide that it is actually a handbook of taxidermy. The book inspires you to take up stuffing dead animals with sand and before long your shelves are graced with everything from mice to mink, from rats to rabbits, each gazing at you with glass eyes and rictus grins. Now one evening, some months after we have both finished the book, we bump into each other at The Slug and Kipper, our local watering hole. Over a pint of Old Peculier, we discover our differences regarding *The God Delusion* and a loud argument ensues over who is right.

"It's a cookery book!" I cry.

"Get stuffed; it's about taxidermy!" you retort. Mid-argument, who should walk in the door but Richard Dawkins himself.

"What are you arguing about?" he asks, in his crisp Oxford accent. On hearing our explanation, he replies: "Well, let me solve it for you: after all, *I'm* the author." Of course, if he's right (and the author's photograph on the back cover suggests he is), then Richard does indeed have the right to determine the meaning of the book. Occasional postmodern protests to the contrary, there *is* such a thing as authorial intent. But, on the other hand, if there is *no* author, if *The God Delusion* were simply created by somebody casually lobbing a hand grenade into the Scrabble™ factory, the letter tiles falling in such a way that they created the text by sheer fluke, then there is no "meaning" in the book, only what you or I choose to read *into* it.[223] And while we can read into it whatever we like, claiming that we have found *the* meaning is utter nonsense, mere braggadocio. Of course, what goes for books goes for the universe too. No God, no author, no meaning, no purpose.

⌘

Over the years, wiser and more thoughtful atheists who have pondered the question of life's meaning have been willing to admit that they have a problem in this area. For example, Bertrand Russell, in one of his most famous essays, wrote:

> Man is the product of causes which had no prevision of the end they were achieving; that his origin, his growth, his hopes and fears, his loves and his beliefs, are but the outcome of accidental collocations of atoms; that no fire, no heroism, no intensity of thought and feeling, can preserve an individual life beyond the grave; that all the labours of the ages, all the devotion, all the inspiration, all the noonday brightness of human genius, are destined to extinction in the vast death of the solar system, and that the whole temple of Man's achievement must inevitably be buried beneath the debris of a universe in ruins … Only within the scaffolding of these truths, only on the firm foundation of unyielding despair, can the soul's habitation henceforth be safely built.[224]

---

223 See the discussion in Richard Taylor, *Metaphysics*, Englewood Cliffs, NJ: Prentice Hall, 1983, pp. 100–105.

224 Bertrand Russell, "A Free Man's Worship", available online at http://www3. nd.edu/~afreddos/courses/264/fmw.htm.

Although these are not jolly or optimistic words, I appreciate Russell's honesty. If there is no God, then humankind is not designed, purposed, or planned: there is *nothing* we are *intended* to be. All that we hold dear, all of our dreams, ambitions, goals, and accomplishments are pure accidents of atoms. Furthermore, no matter how high we squirm up the greasy pole of existence, no matter how enlightened we become, all of it – the whole cathedral of human accomplishment – is destined to become no more than rubble, buried beneath the debris of the end of the universe: utterly ruined, pitch dark, cold as death, achingly alone.[225] Given this one and only certainty, our only option, says Russell, is to embrace despair – to use it as the sole foundation on which we can build. Now Bertrand Russell is not alone in these sentiments: more recently, atheist philosopher John Gray wrote: "We cannot escape the finality of tragedy ... there is no redemption from being human."[226] Or, as an atheist friend paraphrased it on Twitter last year: "Atheism says that you will die, your friends will die, your family will die, the human race will die, the universe will die (this is why atheism is not exactly an easy sell)."

This bleakness explains, I suspect, why so many atheists prefer to run from reality rather than stoically embrace it: "I can distract myself from nihilism, I can invent my own meaning, I can create purpose, I can be happy, I can even have cake!" *Cake?* Where did that come from? It came from Alom Shaha, an atheist who believes that cake can save us from despair, or at least illustrate how an atheist might escape it. Napkins at the ready? Here goes:

---

225 Rather like Skegness on a cold February evening.
226 Gray, *The Silence of Animals*, p. 208.

> People seem to struggle with the notion that this life is all
> there is. Many seem to think that if they accept that this
> is it, life has no meaning. A friend once compared this to
> saying that a cake has no meaning once you've eaten it. A
> cake provides you with a pleasurable experience, a focus
> for celebration, a memory, and even perhaps a wish. An
> eaten cake will give you energy. Some of its atoms may
> literally become part of you through the processes that
> are continually replacing the billions of cells in your body.
> Similarly, when you die, your memory and the things you
> did will live on for a while, but your atoms will live on
> for a lot longer, becoming part of other objects in the
> universe.[227]

When I first read this passage a number of questions formed
in my mind. For example, what type of cake? Are we talking
Victoria sponge or fruitcake? Would a scone or a digestive
biscuit suffice instead? And is there a wheat-free alternative
for gluten-intolerant atheist-seekers-after-meaning? Seriously,
though, I'm not sure that we can buy off Bertrand Russell's
devastating conclusion with a slice of Battenberg, no matter
how generous the helping: "Cake or despair? Er, cake, please."[228]
To understand the problem with what Alom is suggesting, it's
worth returning to the question that Deep Thought raised:
what exactly do we think we are asking about when we enquire
about the "meaning of life"? In a book with almost that very
title,[229] professor of psychology Roy Baumeister suggests that,
if we are to tackle the issue of life's meaning satisfactorily, there
are four underlying questions that must be answered first:[230] the
question of *identity* (Who am I?); the question of *value* (Do I

---

227 Shaha, *The Young Atheist's Handbook*, p. 36.
228 With apologies to Eddie Izzard (*Dress to Kill* DVD, 1998).
229 Roy F. Baumeister, *Meanings of Life*, New York: The Guilford Press, 1991.
230 His work is nicely summarized in McGrath, *Surprised by Meaning*, pp. 104–112.

matter?); the question of *purpose* (Why am I here?); and the question of *agency* (Can I make a difference?). It's fascinating to reflect on how many movies, songs,[231] books, poems, and other cultural expressions explore these questions – I'm not really sure it's possible to live an authentic life without having some kind of answer to them. So can we address them simply by sauntering down the cake aisle at the grocery store? Is life really like a box of chocolate Swiss rolls? I think not.

First, let's think about the first of Baumeister's questions, that of identity. Now when it comes to cake, any piece of cake will do. If I have a craving for coconut pie or a desire for Dundee cake, it doesn't matter which slice I take from the plate in front of me; they are identical. Yet when it comes to human life, most of us do not want to be treated this way, as one of an endless series of equally interchangeable entities. "I am not a number!" cried Patrick McGoohan in the cult 1960s TV show *The Prisoner*, and he was absolutely right: we don't want to be labelled, filed, stamped, indexed, or categorized by our nationality, gender, race, or genetic profile. Yet if we follow atheism it's hard to see how we can be anything other than this: if we are just lumbering biological robots, driven by the puppet masters of our DNA who care not one jot about who we are, provided that we reproduce, then it does seem that the question of identity is unanswerable. We are just one of the teeming herd of humanity, just one identical slice of fruitcake on an infinite smorgasbord.

So much for identity. What about the question of value? In his increasingly crumbly cake illustration, Alom seems to suggest that a slice of cake has meaning because of what it can provide: a pleasurable experience, a happy memory, perhaps

231 For instance, it was just ten seconds into Russell Crowe's first song in *Les Misérables* that I found myself asking: "Why am I here?"

even a wish.[232] The problem with applying this to human beings, of course, is that it is thoroughly utilitarian, a philosophy that is deeply troubling because it tends to see human beings as *means* rather than *ends*. You look at me and you don't see the dashing young writer with the charming accent, but somebody who can lend you a five-pound note,[233] introduce you to the right people, help you get a job, or buy double-glazing from you. Most of us, though, want to be valued for *who* we are, not what others can use us for. Of course, if atheism is true, then Alom is probably right and it's hard to see what actual, inherent value we have simply by virtue of being ourselves. A slice of cake, considered purely as cake on its own merits, is worthless; it's merely a random collocation of atoms. So much for value.

Things get even worse when we turn to Baumeister's third question, that of purpose. For Alom, a cake has purpose – it can satiate my hunger, for instance, or give me energy. But those were not purposes the cherry slice picked for itself; they were purposes *I* gave it. Let me illustrate this from another angle. Sitting on my desk is a rock that I found the other day while walking the wrack line at Greenaleigh Sand, a sandy cove nestling below the cliffs a mile or so from where I'm writing. The rock was one of millions that the tide was idly toying with, but something about it caught my eye. I picked it up and turned it over, studying the way that countless waves had shaped the granite and worn it smooth. Warmed by the morning sun, the rock felt comfortable in my hand; the curve of one side fitted snugly in my palm. So I pocketed it and brought it back to

---

232 I often find that cake leads to a wish for more cake. Indeed, so powerfully does cake seem to attract cake that, were there not a balancing force, the universe would surely collapse in on itself as it crossed the Cake Event Horizon. Thus my hunch is that much of the missing "dark matter" that befuddles physicists is actually Pepto-Bismol™.
233 If this book sells well …

my office, and now the rock has a purpose: it's a paperweight, helping keep Alom Shaha's book open at page 36. Of course, the rock did not *choose* that purpose, any more than the cake *chose* to be eaten. Its existence was meaningless, purposeless until *I* picked it up and changed that fact. What goes for the rock goes for us, too, according to atheism. Unless purpose is provided from *outside* us, there is none at all.

So much for purpose. What, then, of Baumeister's final question, that of agency: can we make a difference in the long term? Yes, says Alom Shaha, in the same way that the cake can: just as the fruitcake's atoms become part of us, so our atoms will outlive us, going on to become parts of other things in the universe, just as they were before us. Of course, that presumably means that my atoms aren't really *mine*, are they? They're just passing through, temporarily occupying the space that comprises Andy Bannister on their way to becoming something else. The atoms that are currently occupied in being you may one day end up in a celebrity chef, or another Pol Pot; a food processor or an atom bomb; as part of the dot making up the letter "i" on the second page of a Nobel-Prize-winning novel, or as part of an HIV virus, wreaking havoc in the body of a baby born to a drug-addicted mother in an inner-city slum. Now you probably brought a value judgment to that list as you read it, just as I did when I typed it, but the atoms don't care. Why would they? They're just doing their thing in the HIV virus as much as they're doing their thing in you. Nothing much you can do about that. Reflecting on these kinds of troubling questions, novelist Leo Tolstoy wrote this in his autobiography:

> [This is] a question without an answer to which one cannot live, as I had found by experience. It was:

"What will come of what I am doing today or shall do tomorrow? What will come of my whole life?" Differently expressed, the question is: "Why should I live, why wish for anything, or do anything?" It can also be expressed thus: "Is there any meaning in my life that the inevitable death awaiting me does not destroy?" [234]

There is an old Indian folk tale about a young man who set off to explore a nearby river on a raft. All was going well as he paddled along until he suddenly heard the distant roar of water. Squinting into the distance, he noticed that the river had a rather disturbing, absence-of-horizon look to it: there was a huge waterfall ahead! Frantically he began trying to paddle to one bank of the river, then the other, but each time the current was too strong. He cried for help, but there was nobody to hear him. Finally, he tried paddling upstream and discovered that he could just about hold the raft still, but couldn't make any progress away from the waterfall. So what should he do? How long until his strength gave out and he drifted to his doom? After contemplating this for a few minutes, he came to a decision. He threw his paddle into the river and lay back on the raft, his hands behind his head and a peaceful smile on his face; after all, he had decided, I might as well as enjoy my final ride.

If atheism is true, we are all the Indian on the raft, the penguin on the ice floe. What awaits us – our civilization, our race, our planet, indeed the universe as a whole – is destruction and extinction, no matter what we do. So, for sure, enjoy the ride, but let us at least be honest about where we are heading. (Although, if Alom has brought enough cake and it has

234 Leo Nikolayevich Tolstoy, *A Confession*, Grand Rapids, MI: Christian Classics Ethereal Library, 1998 [1882], p. 16.

THE ATHEIST WHO DIDN'T EXIST

chocolate frosting, we might die of cholesterol poisoning before we're smashed to pieces on the rocks at the bottom.)

⌘

For all the fondant frosting of foolishness intrinsic to Alom Shaha's patisserie parable, there is something we *can* credit him with, and that's his recognition that atheists have a problem: namely that we cannot live as if life is meaningless. No matter how beautiful the rhetoric, Bertrand Russell was simply wrong – you cannot build upon unyielding despair, because, no matter how good your pile driver, you're not going to find bedrock. If your life is of the same value to the universe as that of a gnat, then it matters not how much wealth, fame, influence, knowledge (or cake) you pile up; it will all be rendered meaningless by your demise. The Jewish psychotherapist Viktor Frankl once remarked that "Life is a quest for meaning". Frankl survived the concentration camps of World War Two, an experience that forced him to look long and hard at these questions, especially the question of whether it is possible to find a meaning that can stand up in the face of incredible suffering. Frankl concluded:

> For too long we have been dreaming a dream from which we are now waking up: the dream that if we just improve the socioeconomic situation of people, everything will be okay, people will become happy. The truth is that as the struggle for survival has subsided, the question has emerged: survival for what? Ever more people today have the means to live, but no meaning to live for.[235]

---

235 Viktor E. Frankl, *The Unheard Cry for Meaning: Psychotherapy and Humanism*, New York: Simon & Schuster, 1978, p. 21.

For all the protests of my atheist friends, I believe that Frankl is correct: you cannot live as if the question of meaning is irrelevant or incidental, or can simply be added on to a purely material existence like a side order of whipped cream at the cake shop. Rather, what you need to find is a framework that enables you to answer those questions of identity, value, purpose, and meaning.

I believe passionately that Christianity answers those questions better than any other world view I have investigated, not least atheism, which scarcely gets off the starting blocks. Beginning with identity, Christianity says that you are not an accident, mere scum on the surface of the cosmic pond, but rather that you were fashioned, shaped, and created by the creator God. What about value? Economic theory tells us that something's value is determined by what somebody is willing to pay for it: for instance, my iPhone is valuable because I was willing to pay hundreds of pounds for the convenience of email that chases me wherever I go and the ability to play Angry Birds on the lavatory. Take my iPhone to an island where there is no power, cell-phone signal or WiFi, and it is probably worthless. So what is our value as human beings? Christianity says that God was willing to pay an incredible price for each one of us, the price of his Son, Jesus Christ. That's why we have value. Turning to purpose, Christianity claims that there is indeed a purpose, one baked into reality, and that purpose is to know God and enjoy him for ever. And, finally, what of agency? In his short story *Leaf by Niggle*,[236] J. R. R. Tolkien tells the story of a struggling painter, Niggle, who spends his entire life trying to paint a beautiful picture of a forest, with a vista of mountains and fields in the distance far beyond. But Niggle so desperately

236 The story can be found in J. R. R. Tolkien, *The Tolkien Reader*, New York: Del Rey, 1986.

wants his picture to be perfect that he can never finish more than one leaf on one tree, endlessly obsessing over getting it right. Sadly Niggle is struck by a chill, falls ill, and dies, his painting unfinished. After his death, Niggle arrives in heaven, where as he approaches the edge of the heavenly country he sees a tree. Not just any tree, but *his* Tree, finished and complete, every leaf perfect. Christianity says that we are all like Niggle: that we *can* make a difference if our efforts, our energy, our work are caught up in and with and are part of God's greater purposes. Then our strivings can not merely outlive us, but be revealed as part of something bigger, beautiful, more real; the kingdom that God is building for eternity.[237]

Well, I can hear some protest that this all sounds very lovely, but it doesn't make it *true*. And with that observation, I would agree entirely. If we live in a godless, materialistic, naturalistic universe then there are some implications that flow from this, whether we like it or not. If that's how the universe is, then theism is indeed a dewy-eyed dream, a romantic delusion, a highly impressionistic painting – lovely in its way, but fundamentally *untrue*. But of course, the cake knife cuts both ways, because the same goes for the atheistic claim that there can be meaning and purpose, flowers and unicorns and puppies and happiness – that's not true either. With atheism, there is no cake whatsoever on offer, just the soggy digestive biscuit of grim nihilistic despair.

That said, if the universe really *is* meaningless and pointless, then you and I are here not because of any higher purpose but simply because a long chain of our ancestors managed to reproduce successfully for generation upon

237 I owe this angle on Tolkien's story to Timothy Keller and Katherine Leary Alsdorf, *Every Good Endeavor: Connecting Your Work to God's Work*, New York: Dutton, 2012, pp. 24–29.

generation, stretching unbroken all the way back across four billion years to things that first wriggled in the primordial soup. Yet if this is true, we're faced with an exceedingly puzzling mystery: namely, why it is that we yearn for more? What is it about human beings that makes us the only the creatures who ask "Why"? Give a cow a field of grass and an occasional bull, and she's happy for life. Human beings, on the other hand, seem disconcertingly dissatisfied with just material things. So then, what was it that possessed evolution, normally so thrifty with its juggling of genes, to equip us and us alone among the animal kingdom with desires not just for cake and copulation, but for value, meaning, purpose, and significance? If atheism is true, we are at best biological freaks, whose desires no more map onto reality than do those of a dyslexic cartographer. But what if atheism *isn't* true? What if those desires, those yearnings *point* somewhere: what if there really is a magnetic north to which the compass needle of the soul is inexorably drawn? To entertain that thought as an atheist may be disquieting, but if you try to chase it from your mind, you hit a worse problem: namely that, if atheism is *true*, not merely is there no meaning to which those desires connect, but the very fact that we have them at all would make us fundamentally irrational – poor, mad, deluded creatures. Evolution has sent us careering down a blind alley, even played a spectacularly sick joke upon us. But if we are *that* mad, *that* irrational, *that* demented, then we cannot trust *any* of our instincts, not one of our desires, none of our most cherished beliefs. Including our belief in cake, hope, meaning, or even in atheism.

For Further Reading

Viktor E. Frankl, *Man's Search For Meaning: The Classic Tribute to Hope from the Holocaust* (London: Rider, 2004)

Os Guinness, *The Long Journey Home: A Guide to Your Search for the Meaning of Life* (Colorado Springs, CO: Waterbrook Press, 2001)

Robert Spitzer, *Ten Universal Principles: A Brief Philosophy of the Life Issues* (San Francisco: Ignatius Press, 2011)

Ravi Zacharias, *Can Man Live Without God?* (Nashville, TN: W Publishing, 1994)

10

The Panini Poisoner of Pimlico

(or: Why Everybody Has Faith)

The noonday sun was shining brightly as I sat down in the park to eat my lunch, a cup of coffee balanced on the bench next to me, the *Times* crossword unfolded on my lap.[238] I was looking forward to half an hour of peace and quiet, watching the ducks and the joggers, but it was then that I saw him.

"Alex?" I called out.

The man wheeling his bike along the path a few feet away stopped and looked at me.

"Alex? It *is* you!"

"Andy? My word, it's been, what – eight years?"

Alex and I had once worked together in the Psychiatry Department of a large London teaching hospital. He'd left to work in marketing for a snack food company, selling crisps

---

238 I usually manage only one or two clues. I used to have a colleague who would regularly impress the office by completing the *Times* crossword in under fifteen minutes (he'd use an old-fashioned stopwatch to time himself). All was awe and wonder until one day somebody retrieved a copy of his newspaper from the wastepaper basket and discovered he'd simply been writing in any old words that would fit.

and peanuts to the pub trade; as he had put it at the time, this wasn't much of a career change – he was still dealing with mixed nuts.

"Hey, grab a seat," I said, moving my newspaper and coffee aside. As Alex sat down, I couldn't help but notice that he was looking dreadfully thin. "Is everything OK?" I asked. "You've lost a few pounds since last time I saw you."

"Not eating well," he said, eyeing my lunch bag. I wondered if he'd fallen onto *really* hard times.

"Chicken and bacon panini," I said. "Would you like some?"

"Are you *serious*?" he said, in the same kind of tone as if I'd suggested deep-fried aardvark in a bun.

"Lunch is *always* serious," I replied, opening the bag. "Plenty enough to share if you're hungry."

"You haven't heard, then?"

"Heard?"

"About … about …" Alex looked around furtively, either scanning for eavesdroppers or possibly looking for a percussion section lurking in the rhododendrons who could perform a suitable drum roll. "About … the Panini Poisoner of Pimlico".

I unwrapped my sandwich and prepared to take a bite. "Nope."

In one swift move, Alex knocked the panini clean out of my hand.

"What the hell are you doing?" I exclaimed.

"Maybe just saving your life. Look, there's this guy, this anarchist guy, who is randomly poisoning paninis in this part of London. Nobody's safe!"

"Just paninis? That seems a bit particular. Does he harbour some kind of vendetta against Italian breadmakers?"

"He's also poisoning pasta, pancakes, pizza, potato bread – "

"What about non-alliterative food stuffs?"

"I'm *serious*," snapped Alex. "It's terrifying. I haven't eaten *anything* for weeks."

I reached down and retrieved my sandwich from the ground, where it was being pecked by a fat-looking mallard that had waddled out of the bushes.

"Where did you read this? *The Daily Mail*?"

"On the Internet. Are you going to eat that sandwich?"

"Yes ... Well, maybe. At least the part of it that hasn't been somewhat ducked."

"But you can't prove it's safe," protested Alex.

"When did you last eat a decent meal?" I asked. The duck gave me an evil look from the shrubbery.

Alex thought for a moment. "Six weeks ago, I think. I've been too afraid to take any chances."

"That explains why I could use your rib cage as a xylophone. Are you seriously telling me that you're refusing to eat *anything* unless you can 100 per cent prove that it hasn't been contaminated? What about drinking?"

"There's the Coffee Contaminator of Chelsea."

I shook my head in disbelief. "You have got to be kidding me. Well, try supplements or something – "

"The Villainous Vitamin Venomizer of Victoria."

"You're making this *up*!" I cried.

"And you're one bite from disaster," retorted Alex. "I don't know how you can fecklessly chow down on a sandwich without being completely certain that it hasn't been interfered with."

"I'm willing to put my faith in health and safety," I replied, through a mouthful. "After all, we've got enough of the stuff."

"Faith," sneered Alex. "Well don't run crying to me when you're lying stiff in the morgue. No, I refuse to eat anything, drink anything, do anything, unless I can prove – prove, not *trust* – that's it's safe."

A jogger ran past, pursued by a goose.

"The trouble is that you can't *live* that way," I replied. "Sure, I can't *prove* that my sandwich hasn't been poisoned. But nor can I prove, at least not to your satisfaction, that my newspaper hasn't been seeded with anthrax by The *Times* Toxifier of Tooting or that where we're sitting hasn't been liberally dusted with botulism spores by the Bench Botherer of Battersea."

Alex leapt off the bench with a shriek of terror, frantically dusting down his jeans with a handkerchief.

"Look, I was joking," I said. "Come on, sit down. This bench is perfectly safe. Trust me"

"No, no," he said, shaking his head. "This has been very helpful. Thank you for helping me see that things are *far* worse than I realized. I need to go and take a shower." And with that he hopped onto his bike and was off, cycling away down the path among the trees.

I looked at the duck, who was still eyeing my sandwich greedily. "Lucky I didn't mention the Bicycle-Brake Breaker of Bermondsey …"

⌘

My friend's refusal to take things on faith when it came to sandwich safety may sound quirky, but in a way Alex was merely taking to extremes a position that is frequently heard among many atheist writers – the common claim that our beliefs, decisions, and choices must rest solely upon reason and evidence, and that there is absolutely no place for faith in a civilized society. I frequently encounter atheists who tell me passionately that faith is folly, faith is foolishness, or, in the words of Mark Twain: "Faith is believing what you know ain't so." By way of contemporary example, in his book *The End of Faith*, atheist Sam Harris writes this:

> [F]aith is what credulity becomes when it finally achieves escape velocity from the constraints of terrestrial discourse – constraints like reasonableness, internal coherence, civility and candor.[239]

In similar vein, Richard Dawkins, writing in *The God Delusion*, describes faith as "evil", because it stands on absolutely no foundations and thus cannot be argued with. Faith, he says, is based on indoctrination, on brainwashing, on believing things because you're a "dyed-in-the-wool faith-head",[240] on holding on to ridiculous religious assertions not merely *sans* evidence but *sans* reason and rationality; indeed, faith is belief "in the very teeth of the evidence". Ah, there's that word again: *evidence*. For Dawkins and atheists of his ilk, there is a frequent tendency to contrast "faith" (which is for the deluded) with Evidence™ and Reason™. I use the trademark symbols only semi-flippantly, because the game is often played in such a way as to suggest that those words belong solely to atheism. We atheists have evidence, you have superstition; we have scientists, you have goggle-eyed, snake-handling loons; we have *reason*, you have *faith*.

Four years ago there was a large rally that brought together atheists, secularists, and other assorted varieties of sceptic from across America. It was held in Washington, DC and the organizers chose to call it the "Reason Rally". Rarely will people amass in the name of politics, though perhaps for a good cause

---

239 Harris, *The End of Faith*, p. 65.
240 Dawkins, *The God Delusion*, p. 28.

some might dare to assemble; but here 20,000 people rallied for a noun. Joking aside, let's engage in a thought experiment for a moment and consider the single most committed of all those atheists who attended the Reason Rally: we'll name our hypothetical secularist Sidney. Now Sidney is *very* serious about his non-belief: he has all of Dawkins's books (in hardback and softback);[241] he regularly wears shirts with atheist slogans; he even has a Darwin fish sticker plastered to his Buick to annoy his Presbyterian next-door neighbour. Sidney is super-keen. Thus, when he heard about the Reason Rally, Sidney was among the very first to purchase a ticket, even being willing to fly all the way from Arkansas for the event. But, as Sidney stood in a field with thousands of like-minded freethinkers,[242] listening to Bill Maher sock it to religion with polemical right hooks, a thought suddenly occurred to him. A worrying thought, a disturbing thought, a deep thought – and this was it: *How do I know that these thousands of other atheists really exist*? Maybe they were figments of Sidney's imagination, especially if he'd been nibbling the Roquefort the previous night. Perhaps they were biological automata, with no minds behind their eyes, merely pretending to be human. Certainly that cute blonde girl he'd tried to chat up at the Atheists for Macramé booth at lunchtime had given him a particularly vacant look when he'd tried out half a dozen of his best chat-up lines on her. What if there really was nobody here other than him and the auditorium was merely one vast echo chamber? Sidney tried to shrug this thought off and tell himself that this was too far-fetched, that he'd been watching too many reruns of *Star Trek*.[243] But then he remembered

---

241 Along with a framed copy of the restraining order after that unfortunate little stalking episode when he visited Oxford three years ago.

242 "Like-minded freethinker" probably has to be an oxymoron.

243 Forty-seven times in the case of the *Star Trek: The Next Generation* episode

something his philosophy professor had said to him back in college: that the so-called "problem of other minds" is one of the most intractable problems in philosophy – we've simply no way of *proving* that anybody else actually possesses a mind, a consciousness, and a thought life like ours; we have to take it on *faith*. Faith? Ugh!

All of this this troubled Sidney, so he tried to distract himself by laughing riotously at Maher's next joke. But then another thought suddenly occurred to him: *How do I know that any of this is real*? Maybe he was just a brain in a jar on a laboratory bench in Idaho, with a mad scientist tickling his synapses with electrodes in such a way that Sidney only *believed* that was Bill Maher up there on the video screen. Or maybe he was hallucinating the whole thing; that mushroom omelette he'd bought from that street vendor yesterday had certainly tasted a little bit peculiar. How could he know that any of this was real? Again, the face of his old philosophy professor swam before his mind's eye, saying: "You can't, Sidney; you have to take it on faith."

By now, Sidney was getting increasingly disturbed and he began to wish he'd never audited that philosophy class. If only he'd taken anthropology instead, or maybe even macramé – then at least he'd have something he could have chatted to that blonde chick about. Sidney needed something to distract himself from further difficult thoughts, so he began to think about how he was looking forward to getting back home tomorrow and seeing his cats. He smiled, too, when he remembered that Richard Dawkins's new book on evolution was sitting on his nightstand waiting to be read, another atheist literary triumph socking it to those dribbling creationist corn-pones who think

---

"Remember Me", as Sidney had a thing for Dr Beverly Crusher.

that the earth is just a few thousand years old. But then, darn it to heck, a further troubling thought popped into Sidney's brain: *How do you know that the world is ancient? Perhaps it just winked into existence five minutes ago, like something from a Lawrence Krauss fantasy, complete with an appearance of age and all of your false memories of the past?* Sidney chewed his nails nervously as he pondered this – after all, he would have no way of knowing, would he? The entire sweep of history could be as fictitious as a Dan Brown novel but he would have no possible means of proving this. Sidney suddenly realized with a shudder that he had but two options: either to be a thoroughly consistent sceptic and accept he could know nothing, trust no one, and take nothing for granted, not even his own existence and personal history, or – well, he had to exercise a little *faith*.

Sidney didn't like where any of this was leading. "Pull yourself together, man," he muttered under his breath. He'd heard Richard Dawkins make rude remarks about philosophy and this was obviously why: it just led to troubling questions. After all, nobody *really* worries about questions like these, do they? (At least, nobody who wrote the kind of books that Sidney liked to read.) He could get through life without faith, thanks very much. In his pocket, his iPhone vibrated and Sidney pulled it out to see a text message from his bank, reminding him to pay his credit card bill. The balance was eye-wateringly large, as he'd had to pay for the hotel and his conference ticket. Then something occurred to him: he'd booked his ticket online, typing his credit card details into PayPal without a moment's thought. But what if nefarious criminal elements had tapped his phone line, waiting to steal his Visa number? What if the bank hadn't screened their staff properly and all their IT department were really money-laundering illegal immigrants?

This was all possible, but none of it had stopped him – he'd used the Internet and the international banking system in faith. Furthermore, Sidney also realized he'd bought a plane ticket and flown across the country without personally screening the pilot, breathalyzing the co-pilot, reading the maintenance logs for the Boeing 737 he flew on, or seeking to interview everybody involved in air traffic control between Little Rock and Washington. In other words, Sidney had exercised faith *yet again*.[244] And, of course, while away, he was trusting old Mrs Perlowski who lived in the next-door apartment to feed his cats and water his bonsai tree collection, but was this wise? Maybe right now she was mincing the moggies and shredding his plants, or holding a wild party for other swinging septuagenarians and quaffing his whisky collection. He couldn't be *sure*, could he? He'd asked for her help in *faith*.

Faith. There's simply no escaping it. For all of the sound bites and polemics, for all of the rallies and bus advertisements, even the most ardently committed atheist cannot avoid faith entirely. None of us can. "Faith is the opposite of reason!" may make a great bumper sticker or tweetable moment, but when it bangs into reality – the small matter of how each and every one of us lives, every day, in the real world – it fails spectacularly. Try if you wish to live a totally faith-free existence, but that will require doing nothing, going nowhere, and trusting no one. Far from faith being about "credulity achieving escape velocity", I'm afraid that without faith the rocket of reason will simply squat sulkily on the launch pad, venting noisily but going nowhere. Faith is part of the bedrock of human experience and one on which we rely in a million different ways every day, usually ways we haven't actually thought about until somebody helpfully

244 He'd even flown Delta, which some might say was taking the whole faith thing just a little too far.

points them out to us. Whether it's life's more philosophical questions – the reality of our conscious experience, why science works, the existence of other minds – or whether it's just the mundane everyday realities of life – flying on a plane, undergoing a medical procedure, sipping a latte, using my credit card – every day I exercise faith in numerous little ways. We especially exercise faith when it comes to relationships, simply because we cannot directly know what another person is actually thinking. It's *conceivable* that all of my colleagues are right now plotting against me, busying themselves rifling through my files and bugging my office while I am away. It *could* be the case that all my closest friends are only feigning friendship because my family doctor, a generous type overly concerned about my introverted tendencies, has bribed them to do so. And it's theoretically *possible* that my wife is only pretending to love me, but is secretly in league with the Panini Poisoner of Pimlico, waiting for the first opportunity to smuggle strychnine into my sandwiches so that she can cash in the life insurance policy and move to Marbella. Even if those are extreme examples, the fact of the matter is that every day, in countless ways, we rely on people whose interior motives and desires we cannot actually know. How do we navigate the often choppy waters of human relationships? We exercise *faith*. We place our *trust*.

⌘

I think that this connection between "trust" and "faith" is actually the crucial link that Harris, Dawkins, and many other atheists all too frequently overlook. Yet the clue is actually in the very word "faith" itself, which comes from the Latin word *fidēs*, meaning "trust" and "reliability".[245] What does it mean to *trust*

---

245 It's also ironic that Dawkins, Harris, Dennett et al. would presumably say that they

somebody: why is it that people generally trust their parents, friends, and spouses, but are more hesitant when it comes to used-car salesmen, politicians or journalists?[246] When we trust somebody, are we simply being naïve, or even discriminatory? Should I just flip a coin at breakfast each morning to decide whom I'll trust most that day – Honest Joe the Genuine-Low-Mileage Used-Honda Salesman (who, incidentally, is running for town mayor, after his local newspaper article "Tom Cruise Ate My Hamster" went viral and made him famous), or my wife, to whom I've been happily married for sixteen years? Of course not. I have good *reasons* to trust my wife, because time and experience have led me to believe that she is trustworthy, honourable, generous, and kind.[247] Because of that, I'm willing to exercise *faith*, to place my *trust*, to believe *in* her. My faith in her is not disconnected from the evidence; it's precisely *because* of the evidence. Faith and evidence are thus closely connected – or, to put it another way, our belief *in* something or someone flows from our belief *that* they are trustworthy.[248]

The problem for those who wish to rally around cries of "Yay for reason! Boo to faith!" is that no amount of sheer facts will ever wholly bridge the gap between knowledge and total certainty, between "belief *that*" and "belief *in*". For instance, I can accumulate fact after fact about my wife, I can gain more and more reasons to trust her, but I can never 100 per cent prove that she isn't a very clever confidence trickster, out to

are confident that atheism is true. Why is this ironic? Because the word "confidence" comes from the Latin *con fidēs* – "with faith".

246 According to a Gallup poll undertaken in 2012 and reported on in *The Huffington Post*, those are among the least trusted of all professions. Of course, that article was written by a journalist, so presumably we can't trust it ...

247 And long-suffering.

248 This different-but-related connection between "belief that" and "belief in" is helpfully teased out by Gregory E. Ganssle, *A Reasonable God: Engaging the New Face of Atheism*, Waco, Texas: Baylor University Press, 2009, pp. 39–42.

play the long game. Likewise, you can never be entirely sure that the plane you're about to catch hasn't just been serviced by a postmodern mechanic who has rewired the entertainment system to the flight computer, such that the first time somebody chooses to watch a Tom Cruise movie, the result will be a smoking wreck. You can accumulate all the *facts* you like about the airline, its safety record, the average height of actors in movies being watched just before planes fall from the sky – a veritable dragon's hoard of glittering factoids – but none of them will get you to utter certainty. There comes a point when you have to exercise *trust*; in short, faith is based *on* the facts, for sure, but must also move beyond them to commitment.

Imagine for a moment that I am hiking in the Lake District. I've only a few hours to spare, so I decide to climb Raven Crag, a vertiginous eruption of rock overlooking Thirlmere reservoir. As I clamber around on the summit, seeking the best angle for a photograph of Helvellyn, I stumble on a wet pine root and slip over the cliff edge. Now as I plummet through the air, soon to become acquainted (briefly but intimately) with the ground far below, I notice a small but sturdy-looking tree jutting out of the rock face. Amateur botanist that I am, I instantly recognize it as an example of *Sorbus aucuparia*, the rowan tree: a plant known for its strong, sappy branches. I have climbed many rowans in my time and recall how they were easily able to bear my ample weight. Furthermore, back in high school I took a few engineering classes and so am able instantly to estimate the load that the tree should be able to carry. (I also know my weight and the rough speed at which I am falling,[249] enabling me to calculate the forces involved.) All of these facts may be fascinating and wonderful, but here's the thing: none of

---

249 Far too fast.

them, no amount of sheer *data* about that tree, will save me from becoming a small, pizza-shaped stain on the rocks below, unless – and only unless – I reach out and grasp that stubby little rowan with all of my strength. What I *know* can't save me; rather, I have to put my facts to the test and exercise my faith. Now what goes for the tree goes for everything else in life. Facts without faith are causally effete, simply trivia, mere intellectual stamp-collecting. That goes too, incidentally, for faith in God. As a Christian, I firmly believe that it's not my faith *as faith* that matters, as much as *whom* my faith is placed *in*. A Christian is not somebody who keeps a tea chest full of doctrines in their mental attic, each one filed alphabetically and regularly polished; rather, a Christian is somebody whose life has been shaped by how they have *acted* on those beliefs. "Here are reasons why God is trustworthy," says the Bible, "from his character to how he has acted in history, especially in Jesus. Now, on that basis, on that *evidence*, will you trust him?"

I'm well aware that, for some readers, the audacity of my including not merely the words "faith", "reason", and "evidence" but also "God" in the same paragraph may seem a lot to swallow. But, contrary to the New Atheist narrative, Christianity has never seen blind faith as a virtue: "Always be prepared to give [a] … reason for the hope that you have," says the New Testament.[250] So how precisely might that work? Well, in exactly the same way as we proceed in most other areas of life, most of the time. "Proof", in the sense that some atheists mean it, brandishing the word around triumphantly like a child with a plastic pirate sword at a fancy-dress party, actually exists only in the realm of logic and mathematics. Certainly, I can *prove* to you that two plus two is four, I can *prove* to you

---

250 1 Peter 3:15.

the law of non-contradiction,[251] but beyond that I can't *prove* much at all, not even that Richard Dawkins exists. In everyday life, we worry less about "proof" and take a more *reasonable* approach: what we tend to do is to weigh the evidence and see where it points.

Imagine that my friend Daniel and I are about to take a hike in the woods a few hours north of my home in Toronto. I'm excited about the hike, not merely as it affords a chance to escape the city,[252] but because I believe that living deep within these woods are a creature I've been longing to see: beavers. Famous as Canada's national animal,[253] beavers were once almost hunted to extinction in Ontario, but have slowly re-established themselves. I believe that there are beavers living in these woods. Dan, though, is a sceptic and disagrees.

After a few minutes' hiking from the trailhead I suddenly point to the ground and call out to Dan: "Look! Beaver scat!" He wanders over and stares at the small pile of dung.

"Nah," he says, shaking his head. "Those are the droppings of the Lesser Spotted Maple Mouse."

I am unconvinced that such a rodent even exists, let alone could pass poop like that, but I let it be and we walk on. A few minutes later, we see some trees by the side of the trail that have been gnawed, clearly bearing the signs of tooth marks. "Aha!" I exclaim. "Beavers have chewed these trees!"

Dan studies them carefully. "I disagree," he says. "That was

---

251 Not to be confused with the Law of Nun Contradiction, which was what my wife learnt at the Catholic high school she attended.
252 Toronto, alas, is blighted by having been largely designed by architects beholden to the idea that if it isn't square and made of concrete, it isn't architecture. If you're British and have never visited Toronto, just imagine the illegitimate offspring of Slough and Hemel Hempstead and you'll get a rough idea.
253 That's national confidence right there. America chose the mighty eagle, Ethiopia chose the brave lion, Greenland chose the ferocious polar bear, but Canada chose the – er, toothy – beaver.

the work of rabbits. Tall rabbits, with really strong teeth."

Once more we walk on and after ten minutes come to a clearing in the woods, in the middle of which stands a lake with what appears to be a beaver lodge in it. The lake itself has been formed by a roughly made dam of logs and sticks thrown across a small stream. "What more evidence do you need?" I ask. "Beavers!"

Dan stares thoughtfully at the scene before us. "There were heavy rains last month, weren't there?" he says. "I think a flash flood swept through here, depositing those sticks in such a way that you *think* it's the work of beavers; but it's just natural detritus."[254]

Well, I was entirely unable that day to convince Dan that there were beavers living in those woods. But we did see a number of pieces of evidence, things that individually might not have been convincing but which, taken *together*, pointed strongly to the conclusion that I was correct. Indeed, on every occasion, too, notice how Dan had to appeal to *ad hoc* explanations: unknown species of mouse, enormous rabbits with great dentistry, freak floods, and such like. In contrast, The Beaver Hypothesis could accommodate all of the data, drawing it together into one cohesive explanation; it's where the *weight of the evidence* lay.[255]

So how might this apply to the God question? Well, in two ways, I believe. First, we need to ask the right questions. Rather than sophomoric sound bites ("Prove God exists, you dyed-in-the-wool faith-head!") we need to be willing to weigh a wide range of evidence and consider where it points when it is *taken*

---

254 Nature abhors a vacuum.
255 I owe the seed of this illustration to Randall Rauser, "Beavers, Beaver-like Creatures, and Ad hoc hypotheses" on his blog at http://randalrauser.com/2012/07/beavers-beaver-like-creatures-and-ad-hoc-hypotheses/.

together. Among the data we would want to consider would be questions such as why there is something rather than nothing; why the laws of physics appear so finely tuned for life – indeed, why there are laws of nature at all and why mathematics so perfectly describes them;[256] why reason and rationality work, why it is that we find ourselves conscious and able to trust our cognitive processes.[257] We would also want to consider questions like beauty and meaning, purpose and morality, and ask ourselves whether the existence of all these things *fits better* with the claim that the universe is, at root, just dumb, mindless atoms banging together, or with the idea that there is some kind of higher power, some kind of God, behind it all.[258] It can be helpful to draw up three columns on a piece of paper and head them "For God", "For Atheism", and "Neutral"; then, as you weigh the data, you can list them under the appropriate column. Here's an example: consider "evolution", often wielded as a stick to dip in lemon juice and poke theists in the eye with. For all of the posturing, however, that probably belongs in the "Neutral" column. After all, if there is a God, presumably he can choose to work through whatever processes he wishes to, right? OK, then, let's try another: what about "evil"? Isn't its existence highly problematic, if an all-powerful, all-good God exists? OK, maybe for now you might wish to choose to write that under the "For Atheism" column (with a footnote to the effect that, if atheism is true, calling anything "evil" is problematic, as all we really have are assorted personal preferences, just a bag of assorted pick-and-mix from the moral candy store). Lastly

256 See Paul Davies, *The Goldilocks Enigma*, London: Penguin, 2007.
257 See Mario Beauregard and Denyse O'Leary, *The Spiritual Brain: A Neuroscientist's Case for the Existence of the Soul*, Toronto: HarperCollins, 2007, especially chapters five to six.
258 On the idea of "fittingness", see Ganssle, *Reasonable God*, pp. 161–175.

for now, what about something like "reason"? Far from being atheism's trump card, it's hard to find any foundation for reason if all that fizzing between your ears is merely atoms knocking about. Chemical reactions just *are*; they aren't true or false. So it's hard to escape the conclusion that mind, thought, and reason seem to point somewhere else. Thus "reason" probably belongs in the "For God" column, at least for now. Do you see how this works? The question is not "What's the knock-down argument for or against God?" but, rather, as I fill in these three columns, where does the growing weight of evidence gather?

Being willing to weigh the evidence honestly is a valuable tool for assessing whether something is worth putting your faith in. There's a second way, too, and that's by being willing to put what you *currently* believe to the test. For instance, what books have you read by those who disagree with you? If you're an atheist and the very most you've ever read by a Christian is *The Pop-up Book of Creationism*, all the while lining your bookshelves with well-referenced works of atheism, I suggest you're not really thinking, but living in an echo chamber. One of the toughest experiences of my life came back in the late 1990s, when I first went to a place called Speakers' Corner in London's Hyde Park. Known colloquially as the free-speech capital of the world, it's a place where anybody can stand on a ladder or a soapbox and talk about anything: religion, politics, science, you name it. Crowds of thousands will often come along to Speakers' Corner to watch, to listen, and sometimes to heckle. A friend had encouraged me to go along and try my hand at street preaching and so, with thoughts of "How hard can it be?" naïvely revolving around my mind, I caught the bus to Marble Arch. On arrival at Speakers' Corner, I ascended my stepladder and was faced with a crowd of several hundred, many well practised in the art of heckling, arguing, and taking Christians to pieces. Over the space of half an hour, I had dozens of questions and objections lobbed at me, most of which I had never even thought about before, let alone had answers for. I remember getting down from the ladder that Sunday afternoon, my head spinning, thinking that everything I had previously held to be true was probably wrong. That night, I lay awake in bed tossing and turning; finally, at around 3 a.m., my long-suffering wife poked me in the ribs and asked what was up. When I told her, her sage advice was: "Maybe you should read a book. Ideally in the morning." And so the following day that's what I did; I went to the local bookstore, purchased my first book of philosophy, and since then haven't stopped reading. I found answers to most of the questions, encountered a whole lot of other questions, but also discovered the thrill of engaging with writers who don't necessarily agree with my convictions, but who hold widely differing views. For all of the fun I poke at Professor Dawkins, I do value him and his fellow New Atheists for forcing me to think. Thus my challenge to my sceptical friends is whether they are similarly willing to critically examine their own assumptions and beliefs. After all, it's only when you're willing to go down to the basement with a flashlight and poke around your foundations that you can really know whether what you're building stands on rock, sand, or simply hot air.

⌘

Yet the question isn't simply one of what foundations your house sits upon, but of what kind of home you wish to inhabit in the first place. A few years before his untimely death from cancer, atheist Christopher Hitchens took part in a panel discussion at the Christian Book Expo in Dallas. During the dialogue, Hitchens made a fascinating statement:

> The struggle is to realize that whilst there is a transcendent and a numinous accessible to us through our imagination – I would give the examples of love, susceptibility to music, landscape, poetry architecture, and so forth, there is no need for this to become a supernatural – especially not a supernatural that contains a hidden but unalterable supervising, superintending, intervening deity.[259]

Douglas Wilson, a Christian pastor who was also on the panel, picked Hitchens up on this: "So on what basis, then, does the transcendent come to exist?" Hitchens didn't like this question at all, demanding to know why it was that if atheists didn't have the supernatural, they couldn't have music, art, landscape, poetry, and the transcendent. This was Wilson's response:

> You can't use the word "transcendent" without explaining "transcends *what*". On naturalism, the space–time continuum is all there is. Our imaginations bump our heads on the ceiling. There is no way to get out. *There simply is no upstairs.*

That is the key point: if atheism is true, if we can believe only that which we can *prove* – in the very strictest, most mechanistic sense of the word – then we are living in a bungalow whose ceiling is very low indeed. Every time we try to ask a deeper question, or appeal to anything outside the realms of physics, chemistry, and biology (realms whose borders are patrolled by

---

259 The video of the discussion can be seen on YouTube at http://www.youtube.com/watch?v=bphSDKOIE6I.

fearsome-looking guards with moustaches and baseball bats), we are stuck, bumping our heads on the ceiling. God? *Ouch.* Morals? *Damn.* Beauty? *Yikes.* Meaning? *Whack!* Philosophy? *Hey, easy with that bat; that hurt.* Play this game for long enough and the head injuries pile up until finally, like one of Pavlov's dogs, you simply learn not to ask the questions in the first place. This is the situation on many of our university campuses, where many students I meet are wary of even raising some of the big questions of life, for fear of flying brickbats from the podium. Yet the fact remains that those things that *really* matter most to us, that define us as humans, all require more than reason – including reason itself.[260] So why is it that many atheists wish to stop at reason, erecting barriers across the road at that point and claiming that all that lies beyond are badlands full of potholes and bandits, with neither gasoline nor a Dairy Queen for 10,000 miles? I wonder if it's because they don't want to admit that reason might be subject to constraints. Often when a person proclaims that Reason is King, what they really mean is *my* reason is on the throne. "We must be freethinkers!" (by which I mean you must all be free to think like me). But if reason has limits, that means that I am not autonomous; maybe I am not "the captain of my soul" but merely a shipmate; maybe there is something before which reason must bow. To what kind of thing might reason need to submit? Well, morality for starters: after all, being the brightest person in the room does not necessarily guarantee that you are safe, sane, or good. It's sobering to reflect that many of the architects of the Third Reich had incredibly high IQs; measured *by intellect alone* they were off the charts. But were they good? Were they moral? When reason tosses morality off the cart and

260 See Douglas Wilson, *The Deluded Atheist*, Powder Springs, GA: American Vision Press, 2008, pp. 24–29.

gallops away with the horses, woe betide anybody who stands in the way.

But faith, too, can be dangerous, I hear many protest. And with that, yes, I wholeheartedly agree. As I read the many examples that Hitchens, Harris, and others have assembled of what happens when religious faith goes wrong, I find myself thinking that the New Atheists have done us all a tremendous service. No wonder many are afraid of "faith" when the word has become attached to mad mullahs, foam-flecked fundamentalists, self-righteous simpletons, and judgmental jihadists. Who would not want to cringe, to fall back, to shout: "A plague on all your houses!" But the problem is there's no neutral ground to stand upon to make that judgment call, for all of us are living by faith. All of us must place our trust in *something*, for humankind cannot live by facts alone. I sometimes suspect that many of the New Atheists believe that if only humans could be more like computers, simply processing facts – churning them over mechanistically in the steely cold light of science and logic – then the world would be a safer place. Maybe it would, but I doubt it. For computers, of course, are everything that humans are not – including being utterly irrational, entirely amoral, and fundamentally stupid. You can programme a computer to respond to the question "What is 2+2?" with "4" or the words "a wet kipper", and it will not know the difference, nor will it care; computers do precisely what they are told to do by their programming, deterministically following their instructions, whether that commands them to add two numbers correctly, print nonsense, display an image of the *Mona Lisa*, or fire a nuclear warhead at Moscow. By contrast, human beings are so much more than this. We have logic, for sure, and it is important. But we also have reason and thought; instinct and feeling; love

and morals; ethics and beauty and truth and subjectivity; and –
yes – access to the transcendent. And on the basis of *all* of that
evidence, not just those bits we can squeeze into a test tube,
we can do that which is fundamentally human, that which no
machine has or will ever be able to do: we can place our trust
somewhere; we can exercise faith.[261] The question is not *whether*
you have faith. You do; we all do – the atheist and the theist, the
sceptic and the seeker, the doubter and the disciple. Rather, the
question is simply this: is that in which you are placing your
faith able to bear the weight; is it trustworthy?

For Further Reading

Anthony Esolen, *Ten Ways to Destroy the Imagination of Your Child*
(Wilmington, DE: Intercollegiate Studies Institute, 2010)

Gregory E. Ganssle, *A Reasonable God: Engaging the New Face of
Atheism* (Waco, Texas: Baylor University Press, 2009)

Kelly Monroe Kullberg, *Finding God at Harvard: Spiritual Journeys of
Thinking Christians* (Downers Grove, IL: IVP, 2007)

Roger Scruton, *The Face of God: The Gifford Lectures 2010* (London:
Continuum, 2012)

---

261 See Clifford Williams, *Existential Reasons for Belief in God: A Defense of Desires
and Emotions for Faith*, Downers Grove, IL: IVP Academic, 2011.

11

The Reluctant Eunuch

(or: Why We Really Can Know a Lot About Jesus)

"You believe you might be *who*?" I said incredulously. The Natural History Museum was full of noisy parties of excited schoolchildren that morning, so I was unsure I had heard correctly.

"'Whom'," my friend Robert corrected. He paused to remove his horn-rimmed glasses and mop his forehead with a handkerchief.

"Look, enough of the pedanticism; are – "

"The word is 'pedantry.'"

" – are you seriously telling me that you believe you might be – "

"Alexander the Great's chief eunuch? That's what I said, yes. I woke up last Wednesday, the thought popped into my head, and I haven't been able to shake it since."

I stared down from the balcony where we were talking at the huge *Diplodocus* skeleton that dominated the museum's entrance lobby. I imagined that it had heard a few things in its time, but this must have ranked as among the most peculiar.

"Why?" I exclaimed. "Not least, if you're going to go for in for wacky Eastern beliefs like reincarnation, why not be Alexander himself?"

"Reincarnation?" sneered Robert. "Don't be ridiculous. No, I'm worried that I actually *am* Alexander the Great's chief eunuch."

"Have you completely lost it?"

"Well, being a eun – "

"You're nuts!"

"Well, again, being a – "

"But that would make this the mid-300s BC."

"How do you know that it *isn't*?" replied Robert, coolly, peering over his spectacles. "You see, here's my problem. The other night, I went to bed with a rather nice bottle of Black Stump Durif Shiraz, a large plate of Stilton, and a copy of *The Sceptic's Guide to Historiography*. The whole lot fermented during the night, which is where I guess the rot set in, and when I woke up – poof! There I was, fretting that I was Alexander the Great's chief eunuch." Robert looked genuinely worried. "Suppose that the book is right! What if the entirety of history is unreliable, untrustworthy, unknowable, and written by the winners as propaganda? That means we can know nothing, trust no one, be certain about *nothing*."

"But we're in a *history* museum, of all places! We have records – "

"Forged."

"Manuscripts!"

"Copied by unreliable scribes."

"Inscriptions!"

"Carved centuries after the events, by people who weren't

eyewitnesses, and paid for by the ruling classes who all had an agenda. Of *course* the Babylonian kings are going to tell you they were the best thing since sliced ciabatta – it's propaganda, nothing more, nothing less."

"But Alexander the Great's chief eunuch? Come *on*, Robert!"

"Once you realize that *all* of history *could* be a fiction, then you realize you have no good reason to believe *any* of it, including your own personal history. So why *can't* I be the harem-keeper of the king of Macedon?"

"Well, for a start, do you live your life surrounded by beautiful women?"

"There's old Mrs Konstantopoulos at number six and those two Greek exchange students in the neighbouring flat."

"The ones who told you that if you knock on their door again they'll call the police?"

Robert polished his spectacles thoughtfully and leant against a display case. From behind the glass, a stuffed dodo stared at us beady-eyed with an expression that said: "You think *you've* got problems?"

"Look," he whispered after a while, "Maybe the issue isn't so much that I think that I *am* Alexander the Great's chief eunuch, but the question of whether I can really know that I'm *not*."

"Well, for a start, if history is as utterly unreliable as you say, that would make everything we believe one vast conspiracy."

"Perhaps it is."

"It would mean that millions – billions – of people down through the ages have been deceived."

"Maybe they have. Often strung along by historians and academics with axes to grind and books to sell."[262]

---

262 Or both, in the case of Henry J. Kauffman, *American Axes: A Survey of Their Development and Their Makers*, Morgantown, PA: Masthof Press, 2007.

I wanted to bang my head in frustration. "OK," I said, "here's one last thought: Alexander the Great's chief *eunuch*, you say? Well, have you – how can I put this delicately – have you actually *checked* whether, er, you – "

"Can sing soprano?" exclaimed Robert. "Now why didn't I think to check that?"

⌘

The idea that history is largely unreliable, a wholly untrustworthy concoction of lies, mistakes, and biases, liberally dosed with layer upon layer of interpretation and marinated in conspiracy, is more common than you might imagine. A few years ago, I spoke at Queen's University in Ontario, giving a lecture on the historical Jesus and what makes him unique when compared with Muhammad, Buddha, and the founders of some of the other world religions. At the end of my talk, there was a question-and-answer time during which a student came to the microphone and said this: "Everything you have said this evening, Dr Bannister, sounds wonderful, but there is just one problem. You are assuming that history is reliable. But I don't believe that it is. We cannot know *anything* about history, and therefore we *cannot* know anything about Jesus. History is just one person's interpretation."

He turned and nodded at the audience, smiling triumphantly like a cat that has got not merely the cream, but the refrigerator, the cows, and the entire milking shed.

"When you say 'history is unreliable', do you mean *all* history?" I asked. "Not merely first-century history, but ancient history, medieval history, modern history?"

"*All* history."

"So that would presumably include reports of this very

lecture?" I asked. "After all, what we currently call the 'present' is shortly going to become 'history'. It's only the second hand of my watch that divides 'now' from 'then' as it sweeps around the dial."

"Well ... I guess so," he said, sounding a little more hesitant.

"In which case, we can't know anything about the conversation we've just had, can we? So if you overhear me in the student bar later this evening regaling people with the tale of how you were so enamoured by my presentation that you renounced your scepticism and became a Trappist monk, you'd be OK with that?"

"But that would be a *lie!*"

"No, it'd just be *my* interpretation of history. It'd be true *for me*. Meanwhile, if you wanted to tell people that you hated the lecture, especially the part where I dressed up as Winnie-the-Pooh and danced the fandango while juggling chainsaws, that'd be true *for you*. We can't know anything about history, I believe you said?"

⌘

The claim that history is unreliable is one frequently appealed to by atheist writers keen to tackle perhaps their central difficulty when it comes to Christianity – namely Jesus of Nazareth. It's one thing to sweepingly dismiss philosophical arguments for the existence of God, or to stereotype all religious believers as deluded, but Christianity hasn't merely put down roots in philosophy, science, and ethics, it's also strongly encamped on history. Indeed, of all the major world faiths, it is really only Christianity that is a "historical" religion, in the sense that history matters to it. Consider this for a moment: if Buddha had never been born, somebody else could have brought the system of thought now known as Buddhism – perhaps Sam Harris could have started it (fond as he is of quoting Buddhist scripture), in which case it might have been called Harrisism instead. Similarly, if Muhammad had never been born, Allah could, presumably, have sent the Qur'an via somebody else; Muslim theology is exceedingly clear that Muhammad was just an ordinary human being.[263] Perhaps, in some alternative reality, Christopher Hitchens was the founding prophet of Islam, although given his reputation for enjoying the quaffing of beverages concerning which the Qur'an is less than enthusiastic, this might quickly have led to complications. But when we turn to Christianity, by contrast, things are a little different, for you quickly discover that Christianity is not a set of teachings brought *by* Jesus; rather, Christianity in a very real sense *is* Jesus Christ – his words, yes, but also his life, his character, his actions, and his very person stand at the heart of the religion.[264]

Given the centrality of Jesus, it is really him that you must tackle if you're going to try to debunk Christianity. After all, for the majority of the world's Christians, what forms the foundation of their faith is not a belief in the validity of Thomas Aquinas's philosophical arguments, but their belief in Jesus.[265] Now, one way to tackle Jesus is to relativize him: this, for example, is the route taken by Islam, with the Qur'an claiming that Jesus was merely a prophet, one whose primary role was to point beyond

263 Even if making that point too clearly in some parts of the world can result in life becoming quite exciting, albeit brief.

264 As my friend Michael Ramsden likes to quip: "Take 'Christ' out of 'Christian' and all you're left with are the letters 'I', 'A' and 'N'. And Ian cannot help you."

265 Which is why it is astounding that, in his chapter on "Arguments for God's Existence" in *The God Delusion*, Dawkins has barely a page discussing the life of Jesus versus nine pages on Aquinas. That would be comparable to my writing a book on the history of the theory of evolution and having an entire chapter on Darwin's preference for knitted socks and buttered haddock, meanwhile relegating the whole Galapagos Islands thing to a couple of extended footnotes.

himself to Muhammad. Or you can try to claim that Jesus was really a Hindu guru, the founder of a magic mushroom cult, or *anything* really – anything other than consider the claims that Jesus actually made about himself. Given that none of those approaches really work, some New Atheist writers have tried a different tack: claiming that Jesus never existed in the first place. After all, history is so unreliable, especially way back then in the first century – why, those poor fools didn't have ratchet screwdrivers, microwave popcorn, or Wikipedia – that we simply cannot reliably know anything about anyone, especially not a figure as controversial as Jesus. Thus French atheist Michel Onfray opines that "Jesus's existence has never been historically established", labelling him a "fable", a "fiction", and a "myth",[266] while Christopher Hitchens called the existence of Jesus "highly questionable".[267] The physicist Victor Stenger, a latecomer to the New Atheist bandwagon, goes further still, claiming that "a number of scholars have made the case for the non-existence of Jesus and their conclusions are convincing".[268] Finally, there's Richard Dawkins, who tries to straddle the wide-girthed donkey of scepticism by both claiming that that "Jesus *probably* existed"[269] and then espousing full-blown doubt on the very next page:[270]

> Dan Brown's novel *The Da Vinci Code*, and the film
> made from it, are arousing huge controversy in church

---

266 Michel Onfray, *In Defence of Atheism: The Case Against Judaism*, Christianity and Islam, London: Serpent's Tail, 2007, pp. 115–116.

267 Hitchens, *God Is Not Great*, p. 114.

268 Victor J. Stenger, *The New Atheism: Taking a Stand for Science and Reason*, New York: Prometheus Books, 2009, p. 58.

269 Dawkins, *The God Delusion*, p. 122.

270 Anybody who has any doubts whatsoever about the power of evolution should marvel at just how quickly Dawkins's historical views mutate over less than two paragraphs; one might almost term this "the origin of the specious".

circles. Christians are encouraged to boycott the film and picket cinemas that show it. It is indeed fabricated from start to finish: invented, made-up fiction. In that respect, it is exactly like the gospels. The only difference between *The Da Vinci Code* and the gospels is that the gospels are ancient fiction while *The Da Vinci Code* is modern fiction.[271]

This gets to the heart of the problem for Dawkins: he believes that our primary sources for the life of Jesus, the Gospels, are entirely unreliable. Elsewhere in the same chapter, Dawkins compares the writing of ancient history to Chinese Whispers, that game beloved of children's birthday parties ever since a pincer movement by the animal rights and health and safety crowds outlawed the nail-gunning of tails onto donkeys. You have no doubt seen the game: a group of small children are arranged in a neat line,[272] a phrase is whispered to the first child, and then each child whispers it to their neighbour. The result is that what emerges at the end of the line bears little or no resemblance to the phrase you started with. This, for Dawkins and others, is how ancient history was done: we mustn't think of Thucydides, or Josephus, or Tacitus, or St Luke as carefully interviewing eyewitnesses, reading sources, and weighing the evidence – goodness, no, they were ignorant ancient yokels, relying on what they half-heard, whispered into their ears, after the stories had made their way through a long line of pre-school children, high on sugar and gullibility. There *is* a problem with this thesis, of course: namely that if ancient historians learned their craft at children's parties, in between doing face-painting

271 Dawkins, *The God Delusion*, p. 123.
272 A fun pursuit in and of itself, unless one uses a strong adhesive, or bribery, or both, to speed up the process.

and making balloon animals,[273] that would imply that we cannot trust *any* ancient history. If we cannot know anything about Jesus then we cannot know anything about the Caesars, or Plato, or Alexander the Great, or anybody. Forget the Dark Ages; what we have before the invention of modern recording equipment is the Foggy Shades of Grey ages, a gloomy murk through which we can see nothing, other than perhaps the dim silhouettes of a few toddlers wandering about, bored with the party games and looking for the chocolate cake. Of course, modern technology doesn't actually really solve the problem either, as records can always be destroyed or manipulated, images Photoshopped™, or the truth buried. If anything, the information age has made matters worse, as even the most half-baked opinion can find fertile ground somewhere in the vast quagmire that is the Internet. Look at the wild conspiracy theories that continue to swarm around the death of JFK, the Moon Landings,[274] the 9/11 terror attacks, or the source of Colonel Sanders' original fried-chicken recipe. If Dawkins is right, then *all* history is bunk, whether it's ancient history or even your own personal history. How can you *really* be sure that you can trust your parents when they tell you that you're descended from a long line of basket weavers who can trace their roots back to the Pilgrim Fathers? Maybe there are dark secrets lying in the family closet (and I don't just mean Great Uncle Tom's moonshine and backgammon habit). Historical scepticism is a universal acid, destroying everything it touches.

⌘

---

273 Every one of which would look, of course, like a dachshund.
274 The lack of any Clangers in the television footage from Apollo 11 has always made me suspicious.

Imagine that I were suddenly to reveal that, when not pondering questions of history or philosophy, I have of late become something of an armchair biologist. I have immersed myself in the literature, reading five, even six books, and I have become increasingly convinced that the theory of evolution is bunkum. Charles Darwin was wrong, Edward Wilson was mistaken, Stephen Jay Gould was in error, and Richard Dawkins, well, my thesaurus fails me. Now I don't yet have an alternative theory – although I am increasingly drawn to the idea that every living thing we see around us is actually made from lint, given the ubiquity of the stuff, especially in the belly buttons of the amply-girthed. Call my theory, if you wish, the Survival of the Fattest. Now among the things that you might say to me by way of rebuttal would be to point out the virtual impossibility of finding *any* trained biologist who agreed with me.[275] And you'd be right to point this out, for one major clue that a theory is not merely slightly in error but wildly, palpably, laughably wrong is when the entirety of a scholarly community – those who are trained in the field and actually know what they're talking about – are unanimously aligned against you. No matter how much I protest about conspiracies and vested interests, my lint-based theory is no more going to fly than a hippopotamus with cardboard fairy wings taped to its back. Now when it comes to the historical Jesus, those atheists who wish to deny that he even existed are in precisely the same territory as my amateurish reworking of biology; historian and sceptic Bart Ehrman, in the introduction to his book *Did Jesus Exist?*, explains:

---

275 Not even Dr Karl Kruszelnicki of the University of Sydney, who in 2002 won a prize for a piece of research entitled "Belly Button Lint and Why It Is Almost Always Blue". I'm assuming if lint got out more, it would be less melancholy.

> What I do hope is to convince genuine seekers who really want to know how we know that Jesus did exist, as virtually every scholar of antiquity, of biblical studies, of classics, and of Christian origins in this country and, in fact, the Western world agrees. Many of these scholars have no vested interest in the matter. As it turns out, I myself do not either. I am not a Christian, and I have no interest in promoting a Christian cause or a Christian agenda. I am an agnostic with atheist leanings, and my life and views of the world would be approximately the same whether or not Jesus existed ... But as a historian, I think evidence matters. And the past matters. And for anyone to whom both evidence and the past matter, a dispassionate consideration of the case makes it quite plain: Jesus did exist.[276]

Once you are willing uncritically to believe things contrary to the vast weight of evidence, even to the extent of entirely ignoring the key scholars in a given field, well at that point all checks and balances are gone. Your theory has achieved escape velocity and is now free to orbit wildly in the outer darkness beyond the gravitational pull of reason and evidence. The Moon Landings? Filmed on a Hollywood backlot. JFK? Assassinated by his future self, who had time-travelled from the future.[277] Evolution? Just a theory invented to scare homeschoolers and keep the plastic toy dinosaur industry in business. As an aside, I find it endlessly fascinating that the New Atheists frequently castigate creationists, ripping into them like a *Tyrannosaurus rex* at an all-you-can-eat hog roast, in particular attacking them for their wilful ignorance of the scientific literature. Yet,

---

276 Bart D. Ehrman, *Did Jesus Exist? The Historical Argument for Jesus of Nazareth*, New York: HarperCollins, 2012, p. 5.
277 Watch the 1997 *Red Dwarf* episode, "Tikka to Ride".

when it comes to *history*, you could thumb the bibliographies of the New Atheist literature until paper cuts have shredded your fingers to the bone, but you won't find them citing trained historians or their opinions on Jesus and the Gospels: they are thus the historical equivalent of the Young Earth Creationists they love to criticize.

So when it comes to history, what *can* we say about the Gospels, the four short biographies from which we derive most of our information about the life of Jesus of Nazareth? Well, the first thing is precisely that: they're *biographies*. As regards what their authors were trying to do as they wrote, most scholars are comfortable with the fact that Matthew, Mark, Luke, and John were trying to write history; when one compares the Gospels with other ancient Greco-Roman biographies, there are striking parallels in terms of style and structure.[278] That's an important first step to get right, because if you fail to grasp the genre of a text, you're going to go badly wrong. If I attempt to read a map of London as a romantic comedy,[279] or *The Diagnostic and Statistical Manual of Mental Disorders* as a graphic novel, I am going to end up confused. Similarly, if we fail to appreciate that the Gospel writers were intending to write history, you are going to misunderstand them: for instance, you may make the sloppy mistake of labelling them as "fable" or "myth". The problem with that is spelt out by Francis Spufford:

> But though Jesus's story certainly has some mythic parallels, and acquired some mythic resonances as it became a whole culture's founding artefact, it does not read like a myth. It's the wrong shape, in a number of different ways. For a start, it doesn't happen in the same

---

278 See Richard Burridge, *What are the Gospels? A Comparison with Graeco-Roman Biography*, Cambridge: Cambridge University Press, 1992.

279 The characterization was terrible, but the places seemed so real.

special time set aside for myths, the dream-time, the long ago zone off to the side of calendar history where gods and heroes strutted their stuff. What year was it when Odin hung on the tree? The question does not compute. It's a category error, like asking what colour accountancy is. Jesus's story, by contrast, happens at a definite historical address. As *Monty Python's Life of Brian* puts it, 'Judea, AD 33, teatime'.[280]

When you read the Gospels properly this is one of the things that immediately strikes you: these are documents concerned with dates, times, and locations. On that last point, it's fascinating to observe that the Gospels refer to dozens of place names along with details about them, displaying a level of geographical accuracy that is hard to explain were the Gospel writers simply amateurish hacks knocking out fiction in a rented room above a taverna somewhere, thousands of miles and hundreds of years removed from the events. Fine detail is a key clue: if asked to name the capital of France, even the most poorly travelled southern redneck could probably succeed if he tried *really* hard, but if I asked you to start naming minor villages a hundred miles from Paris, you'd probably struggle unless you'd actually visited the region. Yet that's precisely the level of detail the Gospels get right, managing to know not just major cities such as Jerusalem but minor villages like Cana and Chorazin, one-goat towns in their day. The Gospels also get a wealth of other local information right, from politics to agriculture, economics to weather patterns; they even get people's names right. Names are fascinating things, because names come and go in popularity; while there are always the wacky celebrities who think that calling their child Petal Blossom Rainbow

---

280 Spufford, *Unapologetic*, p. 160.

or Diva Thin Muffin is a clever idea, most people follow the cultural trends. So what names were people commonly calling their kids in the first-century Palestine of Jesus' day? Well you don't need to lie awake at night fretting about the answer to that one, because scholars have done the work, carefully recording in a computer database the thousands of names we know of from the inscriptions, tombstones, and writings of first-century Israel. In 2006, a British scholar called Richard Bauckham, admirably demonstrating the kind of extreme boffinry for which England is legendary,[281] decided to painstakingly cross-check this database with the New Testament. What he discovered was that the naming patterns in the Gospels precisely match those of the period, adding further credence (if any were needed) to the idea that Matthew, Mark, Luke, and John were intimately acquainted with the time, place, and culture that they wrote about; in short, the Gospels have the flavour of eyewitness accounts.[282]

Of course none of that prevents the sceptic from continuing to cry "Phooey!" – perhaps the Gospel writers were simply penning historical novels, the ancient equivalents of *Downton Abbey*. Except, rather inconveniently, the very concept of the historical novel wasn't invented until millennia after the Gospels, when nineteenth-century writers such as Sir Walter Scott popularized the idea of trying to accurately create the world of the past in their fiction.[283] All of this poses the hardened sceptic with a bit of a conundrum: either Mark, the first Gospel writer, managed to invent a brand new literary

---

281 Largely, it must be said, because of the climate. If it were not for the rain and the damp, Britain would probably never have given the world the jet engine, the programmable computer, or the magnetic tea towel.

282 See chapters three and four of Richard Bauckham, *Jesus and the Eyewitnesses: The Gospels as Eyewitness Testimony*, Grand Rapids, MI: Eerdmans, 2006.

283 See Georg Lukács, *The Historical Novel*, London: Penguin Books, 1969.

genre over 1,700 years earlier than anybody had previously thought, or when Richard Dawkins and other New Atheists compare the Gospels to fiction they are guilty of the grossest of anachronisms. This is deliciously ironic, because it is precisely the *lack* of anachronisms that is one of the signs that what the Gospel writers are attempting to give us is history and biography.

⌘

There's a further feature of the Gospels that strongly suggests we are not dealing with fiction, and that's that they are awkward. One of the hallmarks of fiction, of invention, is that it is flexible, malleable, easily bent to the whim of the writer. If you ask me why I'm obsessed with the history of the 1920s British Everest expeditions and I'm free to make things up, why, it's easy: I'm a direct-line descendant of Sir Edmund Hillary. On the other hand, if you boringly insist that I tell the truth, then I have to recount a complicated story involving how I first became drawn to the hills, a wet weekend in Keswick that forced me into a mountain history exhibition, the accidental purchase of the wrong book from an Ambleside bookseller,[284] and later the desire to holiday somewhere more exotic than Southend-on-Sea after my fear of flying was cured. It's a complicated story that takes some telling, but its rough, unhewn edges offer a clue that you're dealing with the truth, rather than fabrication.

We see a similar feature in the Gospels; let me give you one example. Thanks in part to the writings of Paul, historians have a good idea of some of the controversies that raged in the early church shortly after the Jesus movement began in the

---

284 Robert MacFarlane's brilliant *Mountains of the Mind: A History of a Fascination* (London: Granta, 2003), if you must know.

middle decades of the first century. These included the conduct of worship services, the role of women, and, towering above them all, the question of which aspects of the Jewish law had to be kept by Gentile followers of Jesus – in particular, did men have to undergo a certain Jewish procedure that, if carried out too carelessly, certainly might make one a candidate for the role of gatekeeper to Alexander the Great's harem? As you read New Testament books such as Paul's Letter to the Galatians, you get a sense of how divisive the debate that swirled around Gentiles and circumcision could sometimes be. All of which raises a question, doesn't it? If the first Christians were simply inventing the Gospels from whole cloth, then why not put something *really* useful into the mouth of Jesus? Rather than have him say things about the Temple tax (irrelevant after the fall of Jerusalem in AD 70 anyway) or engage in protracted debates with the Pharisees, why not invent a story where Jesus directly answers the circumcision question? Why not concoct an episode in which he clearly sets out how a church service should be ordered, including the choice of hymns and the colour of the post-service coffee cups? Or, quite frankly, if the Gospel writers were simply writing stories to gain power and influence (as one version of the sceptical narrative goes), why doesn't Matthew (a former tax collector, for heaven's sake) possess the gumption to have Jesus announce the many blessings that will be showered upon those who send money to the church – oh, and by the way, here's a forwarding address for the cheques. Rather, in contrast to all of this, the more you read the Gospels and allow them to be themselves, the more a Jesus emerges who was very much his own man, standing wholly within neither the Judaism that preceded him nor the early church that came afterwards. Thus if you insist on thinking that the Gospels are fictitious, you need at least to answer this question: fictions designed to do *what*, precisely?

Then, of course, there are Jesus' own questions. Everywhere you look in the Gospels, Jesus asks questions, or more commonly answers a question with a question,[285] doing so with a fluency that would make the average politician green with envy (although, in Jesus' case, he doesn't usually do it to get himself off hooks, but to make his questioner squirm). A textbook example occurs in the tenth chapter of Mark's Gospel, where a man runs up to Jesus and asks: "Good teacher, what must I do to get to heaven?" Now, were the Gospel writers inventing this story, what a wonderful opportunity to have Jesus give some theologically succinct answer: "Repent of your sins and be baptized." Or, if Mark had one eye on his pension fund as well as his quill, why not: "Send ten drachmas to the apostles" or some other self-serving answer. None of these is even remotely close to what Jesus *actually* says: "Why do you call me good? No one is good – except God alone." Now, quite frankly, were this story the invention of Mark, or the early church, or Ye Olde Jerusalem Presbyterian Writers' Guild, then at this point you would have to politely ask what they were smoking. The early church was, after all, demarcated from Judaism by the very fact that Christians worshipped Jesus as divine; so what possessed them, for Saint Peter's sake, to create stories where Jesus appears to deny his *good*ness, let alone his *god*-ness? Of course, if you read on, things get more interesting, but to say that this story gave the early church fathers a few headaches is to toy lazily with understatement. The best explanation of the story's presence would seem to be that Mark and his fellow Gospel writers were committed to passing on the teaching of Jesus, awkwardness and all.

---

285 See Conrad Gempf, *Jesus Asked*, Grand Rapids, MI: Zondervan, 2003.

Something similar is going on when you consider the ethical teaching of Jesus. People are remarkably fond of commenting on the profundity of Jesus' principles, the sublimity of the Sermon on the Mount, or the wisdom of his morals. "I wouldn't call myself a Christian, but you've got to admire Jesus' ethics" is often how it goes. And, indeed, if more of us lived by the principle of "Do unto others ...", the world would no doubt be a significantly happier place, with considerably cheaper insurance premiums. But what about "Love your enemies and pray for those who persecute you"? "Well, now, hang on a moment, that's going perhaps a bit *too* far. Have you *seen* my enemies? (Come to think of it, have you seen some of my *friends*?) If you knew the people at my workplace, you'd understand – why, one of my colleagues stole my coffee mug just last week" ... "If somebody takes your coat, offer them your shirt too"? "OK, now you're talking nonsense. That's just not *practical*. Look, I'm basically a good person, voted Labour all my life, give to the Salvation Army whenever they rattle a tin outside Tesco, so cut me a little slack, will you?" ... "Be perfect, as God is perfect". "Right, now you've *really* lost it. Perfect? You're *insane*, mister." See the problem we have? Jesus' so-called "moral" teaching goes far beyond a mere code of ethics in much the same way as a Saturn V goes beyond a schoolboy's bottle rocket. Normal ethics, religious or otherwise, says things like keep your nose clean, toe the line, keep this handful of commands, and you'll be OK. If you or I were inventing the Gospels, let's be honest, that's the kind of thing we'd have come up with. Manageable, bearable, doable, workable, and other words ending in "-able". In short: not too onerous. Instead, we have a Jesus who seems to have been as much concerned with attitudes, motives, and thought life as with actions: "You have heard that it was said, 'Do not commit adultery'. Well, I say to you that anyone who even *looks* at another person lustfully has committed adultery with them in their heart." Now what do we do with that? This seems wildly impractical stuff, especially to an appearance-obsessed, desire-fuelling, sex-saturated culture such as ours; in fact, it's *so* bold, *so* outrageous, *so* far beyond a simple moral checklist that one is forced to conclude that it is either, quite frankly, unworkable nonsense, or else it's something quite different entirely.

And then, finally, there are the staggering personal claims of Jesus. Although Jesus never comes out directly and announces: "Lo, I am the Second Person of the Holy Trinity" in a booming voice like Charlton Heston's (which would be the kind of anachronistic language that would cause even Dan Brown to blush), Jesus nevertheless holds very little back: claiming to be able to forgive sins; putting his own words on a par with the Jewish Scriptures; carrying on like a one-man replacement for the Temple; telling stories that portrayed God as a king and him as the king's beloved son; borrowing language and imagery from the Old Testament that implied that he thought much of the scriptural story was about him or pointed to him. Cryptic, you say? Well, arguably not *that* cryptic, given that Jesus pushed the needle far enough into the red zone for the religious leaders of the day to cry "Blasphemy!" as they arrested him and handed him over to the Romans. And not too cryptic for the first Christians – good monotheistic Jews, most of them – to work out, with fear, yes, and trembling, quite definitely, what was going on and whom they were dealing with.[286]

Once again, if we were dealing with theological fiction, one would expect the edges to be straighter, the language more doctrinally polished. Which leaves us with the question: *What*

---

286   See Ben Witherington, *The Christology of Jesus*, Minneapolis: Fortress Press, 1990.

is going on? Or, perhaps more pointedly, who did Jesus *think* he was? The former Oxford atheist C. S. Lewis, when faced with this question, famously coined his "Trilemma": either Jesus was *mad* – on a par with a man who says he is a fried egg, or Alexander the Great's chief eunuch. Nice enough chap, sure, in a Keep-Him-Away-From-Children-and-Sharp-Objects kind of way. Or Jesus was *bad* – a wicked deceiver, out to use religion as a means to gain power and influence. (Of course, if that was the goal, it went badly wrong, didn't it?) Or, says Lewis, if "mad" and "bad" don't work, you're left with the third alternative: that Jesus was *who he claimed to be.* Now, to his credit, Richard Dawkins is at least aware of the force of Lewis's Trilemma and so he tries to wriggle off the hook by suggesting that "a fourth possibility, almost too obvious to need mentioning, is that Jesus was honestly mistaken. Plenty of people are."[287] Now, my life must be considerably less Bohemian than that of Dawkins, for while I have been mistaken about many things, these are usually of the order of the location of the car keys, the date I agreed to hang those shelves for my wife – I think the highest level of mistakenness I have ever managed was when, aged twelve, I was quite badly mistaken about how much black powder one can extract from a couple of cheap fireworks with a penknife.[288] Not once, not ever, not even on a Thursday, have I woken up and decided that I uniquely shared in the divinity of the one, all-powerful, creator of the universe. Indeed, were I to suggest such a thing within earshot of a passing psychiatrist, I suggest that he or she would prescribe something considerably more potent than a nice cup of tea and a sit down. Curious, isn't it, that Dawkins believes that Christians are deluded for believing

---

287 Dawkins, *The God Delusion*, p. 117.
288 The answer: quite a lot. But everybody should blow their eyebrows off at least once in their life.

there *is* a God, whereas he thinks Jesus was merely "honestly mistaken" for believing he *was* God. Maybe there's a good reason that Dawkins chose biology rather than psychiatry as a career path.

⌘

That we're even having this discussion, 2,000 years after the events of Jesus' short public ministry, is itself startling, when you stop and think about it. The point is well made by the famous meditation written almost a century ago:

> He was born in an obscure village, the child of a peasant woman. He grew up in another village, where he worked in a carpenter's shop until he was thirty. Then for three years he was an itinerant preacher. He never wrote a book, never held an office, never went to college, never visited a big city. He never travelled more than two hundred miles from the place where he was born. He did none of the things that usually accompany greatness. He had no credentials but himself. He was only thirty-three when the tide of public opinion turned against him. His friends ran away. One of them denied him. He was turned over to his enemies and went through the mockery of a trial. He was nailed to a cross between two thieves. While dying, his executioners gambled for his clothing, the only property he had on earth. When he was dead, he was laid in a borrowed grave through the pity of a friend … All the armies that have ever marched, all the navies that have ever sailed, all the parliaments that have ever sat, all the kings that ever reigned put together, have not affected the life of mankind on earth, as powerfully as that one solitary life.[289]

---

289   A combination of the original version in James Allan Francis, *The Real Jesus and Other Sermons*, Philadelphia: Judson Press, 1926, pp. 123–124, and that found in Os Guinness, *The Long Journey Home*, p. 158.

Given the inauspicious start and equally inauspicious end to the life of Jesus of Nazareth – crucified on a cross on a Judean hillside by the imperial Roman oppressors – the influence of his life has been nothing short of remarkable; simply labelling the founding stories of Christianity as historically unreliable offers little explanation for why this is the case. The first Jewish Christians claimed that Jesus was the Messiah, but the Messiah was supposed to overthrow and defeat the Romans, not get tortured and executed by them. Indeed, the cross was a tremendous obstacle that the early church faced in their preaching; both Jewish and Gentile audiences poured scorn on the Christians for their belief in a crucified messiah, leading Paul to famously describe the cross as "a stumbling block to Jews and foolishness to Gentiles".[290] If the Gospels *are* fictitious, it is almost as if their authors set out deliberately to create the greatest difficulties for themselves: "Hey, let's claim that Jesus was divine; that'll offend *Jews*!" "Great idea, but let's also call him *Lord*: that'll offend the Romans and get us persecuted for failing to ascribe that title only to Caesar." "What about claiming he was *crucified*? That'll annoy *everybody*."

So what does account for the influence of this one solitary life? One answer, of course, might be the resurrection: had Jesus' followers not claimed he had been raised from the dead, the story would have ended there – Jesus of Nazareth just one more failed messianic claimant among the dozens that litter this small corner of history, his tattered corpse just one of thousands of Jewish victims of the Roman imperial juggernaut. Yet indulge me in one last thought experiment, just for a moment. Imagine, that first Easter morning, that, rather than Jesus, his followers had encountered some other random person risen from the

---

290   1 Corinthians 1:23.

dead – perhaps one of the thieves who had been crucified next to Jesus for petty brigandry. Would the mere fact that there had been a miracle, even one as great as a resurrection, have been enough to launch a whole new religious movement? Arguably not, for the power of the stories of Jesus' resurrection is not found in their describing some random miracle, but is because of *who* it happened to: in short, the resurrection vindicates all of Jesus' teaching that had gone before. The Gospels are not claiming: "Look, people pop back from the dead all the time; Gehenna and Hades are really just like a quick trip down the road to the garage for a packet of cigarettes. Isn't life prior to the scientific revolution wonderful?!" I would suggest that the average first-century person knew far more about death than we do, given the brutal shortness of much of life then. No, the more radical claim of the Gospels is that this *one specific life*, this one, solitary, remarkable, incredible life – this man, uniquely, was raised from the dead. Dismiss this as an invention if you wish, but make sure you know *what* you're dismissing first; and remember, too, that if you throw out the resurrection, you're still left with the huge questions of Jesus' character, teaching, and identity.

And, finally, the question of Jesus brings the whole "God Debate" into sharp focus. Too many of the hackneyed arguments, polemics, and sound bites swirling in the culture wars that the New Atheism has generated have, for me, almost invariably been glorified and extended exercises in missing the point. You see, the question that lies at the heart of Christianity is not "Does God exist?" That may be something that keeps philosophers on either side of the question busy, but my problem with it is that it is way too abstract. The question that Christianity is primarily concerned with, that the Bible wrestles with, that the Gospels explore – through the lens of the life of Jesus – is far more personal than that: it is *What kind of God?*[291] As I read the New Atheists I have this frequent nagging hunch that many of them would, quite honestly, have little problem with the distant God of the Philosophers, an absent, impersonal, animating principle or force, something that breathes fire into the equations of physics and then totters off and lets the universe be. But the God of Christianity, the God of the Bible, the God seen in Jesus is a God who isn't willing to lurk in the shadows, but one who, the Gospels claim, has stepped into space–time and walked into history, who has his nose up against the window and is tapping loudly on the glass, demanding our attention. That's the God whose foot many atheists are, I believe, desperate to keep from getting in the door, the window, the cat flap or *anywhere*. Arguments are thus needed, *any* arguments, no matter how bad, provided we can hammer them like planks across any possible opening. But, as the historian N. T. Wright puts it: "It may be time to be sceptical about scepticism itself."[292] Not least because perhaps, just perhaps, we are more broken and messed-up than we realize – indeed, some of the bad arguments we have explored in this book show us just how little we can actually trust ourselves, however reasonable, ethical, or objective we like to believe we are being. Deep down, I have a hunch that we all know, really, that the deceits we need worry most about are not those allegedly littering the pages of history or even theology, but the lies – the softly spoken, intricately woven half-truths – we tell ourselves about ourselves. But if the Gospels are true, on the other hand, they tell us something even

---

291   See N. T. Wright, "Jesus and the Identity of God", *Ex Auditu* 14 , 1998, pp. 42–56. (Available online at http://ntwrightpage.com/Wright_JIG.htm.)
292   N. T. Wright, *Simply Jesus: A New Vision of Who He Was, What He Did, and Why He Matters*, New York: HarperOne, 2011, p. 58.

deeper, too: through the lens of the life, teaching, cross, death, and resurrection of Jesus they proclaim that all is not acidic scepticism, or unyielding despair, or hopeless lostness, or the utter blackness of the void, but that everything that is broken, including us, *can* be mended. They boldly declare that, if these stories are true, if Jesus is who he claimed to be, then because of his history and in spite of ours we *can* have a future. Perhaps it is time we laid bad arguments aside, even just for a few hours, and gave Jesus a careful, considered look.

For Further Reading

Richard Bauckham, *Jesus and the Eyewitnesses: The Gospels as Eyewitness Testimony* (Grand Rapids: Eerdmans, 2006)

John Dickson, *Jesus: A Short Life* (Oxford: Lion Hudson, 2008)

Timothy Keller, *Encounters with Jesus: Unexpected Answers to Life's Biggest Questions* (New York: Dutton, 2013)

N. T. Wright, *The Challenge of Jesus* (London: SPCK, 2000)

Acknowledgments

The very first seeds of *The Atheist Who Didn't Exist* were planted on 11 May 2001, a date forever etched in my memory, as that was the day that one of my childhood heroes, the humourist and writer Douglas Adams, died suddenly of a heart attack. He was also an atheist, friends with Richard Dawkins, and when I first read Dawkins's book *The God Delusion* I was intrigued to see a quote from Douglas on the dedication page: "Isn't it enough to see that a garden is beautiful without having to believe there are fairies at the bottom of it?" What Dawkins failed to tell the reader was that the quote comes from Douglas' best-selling novel *The Hitchhiker's Guide to the Galaxy*, a book that also fires a few shots at brash and overly confident forms of atheism. For sure, Douglas was an atheist, but unlike some he was generous and knew well the difference between humour, satire, and sheer ridicule.

When it comes to the "God Debate", I think we badly need a fresh dose of humour and satire amidst the ground-shaking thuds of philosophical howitzers being fired from entrenched positions on both sides. Humour is powerful because it can prick pomposity and puncture delusions of self-importance. There have been many times in history when it's been organized religion that has needed this critique: Jesus aimed it at the Pharisees in the first century, just as *Monty Python's Life of Brian* did it to the church 2,000 years later. But now, a decade and a half into the twenty-first century, it's a different fundamentalism that needs deflating: atheism, or at least the New Atheist flavour of it. When you're so convinced of your own self-righteousness, intellectual superiority, and sheer sophistication that your arguments become as bad as some of those I have collected for this book, something has gone badly wrong. I hope that *The Atheist Who Didn't Exist* will encourage you, even if you describe yourself as an "atheist" or an "agnostic", to be somebody who thinks *well* and avoids terrible arguments like the plague.

A lot of people have helped to make this book possible; while space does not permit me to list them all, a few deserve special mention. First, I must profoundly thank Andrew McCausland and Minehead Baptist Church for so generously giving me office space in which to lurk for a summer. Not least because the North Somerset coast is a beautiful place to write, and whenever I needed to clear my head I could walk deserted beaches for miles; strolling the wrack line between the tides where all manner of interesting things await the walker.[293] Next up, I must thank friends and colleagues who patiently acted as sounding boards for some of the material in this book. In no particular order: Simon Wenham, Nathan Betts, Abdu Murray, Stuart McAllister, Carson Weitnauer, Nabeel Qureshi, Jeff Allen, Rick Manafo, and Cameron McAllister. Authors seeking to sound humble often say that they "stand on the shoulders of giants"; given my diminutive stature and the fact that so many of my colleagues are distressingly tall, this is very much the case. Thanks are also due to Tony Collins and his team at Lion Hudson for first believing in this project, commissioning it, and helping to see it to fruition. Finally, I must thank my wife, Astrid, and daughter, Caitriona, for their support and

---

293 Especially if you don't watch where you are putting your feet.

encouragement while I was buried away writing chapters.

Large portions of the book were written to the accompaniment of Kate Rusby's beautiful album *Ghost*, a soundtrack that often helped me to clear my head, refocus, and remember what beauty sounds like.

All that is good, helpful, and true in the book I owe to those listed above and to others too numerous to mention; any faults or shortcomings are entirely down to me.

Text Credits

Extracts pp. 19, 220–21 taken from *Unapologetic* by Francis Spufford. Copyright © 2013 by Francis Spufford. Reprinted by permission of Faber & Faber.

Extracts pp. 28, 49–50, 73–74, 149–50, 215–216 taken from *The God Delusion* by Richard Dawkins. Copyright © 2006 by Richard Dawkins. Published by Bantam Press. Reprinted by permission of The Random House Group Limited, and Houghton Mifflin Harcourt Publishing Company. All rights reserved.

Extracts pp. 32, 101, 126–27 taken from *God is Not Great: How Religion Poisons Everything* by Christopher Hitchens. Copyright © 2007 by Christopher Hitchens. Used by permission of Twelve, an imprint of Grand Central Publishing, and McClelland & Stewart, a division of Penguin Random House Canada Limited, a Penguin Random House Company. All rights reserved.

Extract pp. 69–70 taken from *A Devil's Chaplain* by Richard Dawkins. Copyright © 2004 by Richard Dawkins. Reprinted by permission of Orion Books.

Extract p. 75 taken from "What Shall We Tell the Children?" by Nicholas Humphrey, *Social Research* 65.4 (1998), 777–805. © 1999 New School for Social Research. Reprinted with permission of Johns Hopkins University Press.

Extracts pp. 86, 144, 177 taken from *The Young Atheist's Handbook* by Alom Shaha. Copyright © 2012 by Alom Shaha. Reprinted by permission of Biteback Publishing.

Extract pp. 90–91 taken from *Ends and Means* by Aldous Huxley. Copyright © 1938 by Aldous Huxley. Reprinted by permission of Georges Borchardt, Inc., for the Estate of Aldous Huxley.